BLISSFUL DETOX

OVER 100 SIMPLY DELICIOUS CLEANSING RECIPES

Louisa J. Walters | Aliza Baron Cohen | Adrian Mercuri

LAUREL GLEN

Laurel Glen Publishing
An imprint of the Advantage Publishers Group
5880 Oberlin Drive, San Diego, CA 92121-4794
www.advantagebooksonline.com

ISBN 1-57145-581-7

Library of Congress Cataloging-in-Publication Data

Walters, Louisa J.
    Blissful detox: 100 simply delicious cleansing recipes/Louisa J. Walters, Aliza Baron Cohen, and Adrian Mercuri.
        p. cm.
    Based on: The detox cook. London: Kyle Cathie, 2001.
    Includes bibliographical references and index.
    ISBN 1-57145-581-7
    1.   Detoxification (Health) 2. Cookery, Chinese. 3. Medicine, Chinese. I. Cohen, Aliza Baron. II. Mercuri, Adrian. III. Walters, Louisa J. Detox cook. IV. Title.

RA784.5. W35 2001
641.5 63 dc21   2001023793

Commissioning Editor: Helen Woodhall
Editorial Assistant: Andrie Morris
Copy Editor: Alexa Stace
Home Economists: Pippin Britz and Carol Tennant
Designer: Heidi Baker
Production: Sha Huxtable and Lorraine Baird

Printed in Singapore

1 2 3 4 5   05 04 03 02 01

Note To Readers

This book contains the opinions and ideas of its authors. It is intended to provide helpful and informative material on the subjects addressed in this book. It is sold with the understanding that the author and publisher are not engaged in rendering medical, health, or any other kind of personal professional services in the book. The reader should consult his or her medical, health, or other competent professional before adopting any of the suggestions in this book or drawing inferences from it. The authors and publisher disclaim all responsibility for any liability, loss, or risk, personal or otherwise, which is incurred as a consequence, directly or indirectly, of the use and application of any of the contents of this book.

contents

introduction

When people think of a detox, they think of suffering and the denial of good food, or even no food. The result is a very hungry, deprived, and unhappy person. Not really the emotional detox one would want. As health practitioners, we tend to find that people doing these sorts of detoxes don't stick to them. This book offers a detox that is great tasting and easy to stick to. Use this simple detox diet for the rest of your life, not just for a day or a week!

We have based our relaxed and commonsense approach to detoxing on the dietary therapy of Chinese medicine, which deals with the properties of food and their effects on health and the prevention of disease. It is part of their culture for food to be a friend that is nurturing, helping to maintain and restore health. Quite the opposite from here in the West, where we tend to concentrate more on what is not good for us and become worried about what we eat, so that food becomes our enemy.

Our aim is to give a detox that does not encourage rigidity or denial. Emphasis is on listening to your body and feeding it what it needs, while still creating appetizing meals—usually a daunting task when you are trying to improve your health through changes in your diet. We hope to have made this easier by helping you to determine your body type using the ancient Chinese principles of yin and yang (see questionnaires on page 12–13). Once you have determined if you are a hot, cold, or neutral person, you will be able to detox more efficiently by choosing cleansing and healthy recipes that correlate to your individual needs. This type of detox will leave you feeling healthier and more energetic than ever before.

For example, if you are a cold person and your energy is sluggish and you are always or often tired, you can correct this by eating foods from the warming recipes because they stimulate and increase the body's energy. You may have done a regular detox and eaten lots of the fruit and vegetables mentioned in the cooling recipes of this book. These would have slowed and calmed you down, making you feel even more tired and sluggish.

As holistic practitioners and chefs, we have firsthand knowledge of the benefits our clients have gained when their diet reflects their lifestyle and body type. If you are sick, you need to consult a professional Chinese doctor for guidance in determining your body type, as food is not a substitute for medicine, though it can be a help.

WHY SHOULD I DETOX?

The human body is built to cope with a certain amount of toxins and has its own natural methods of eliminating excess waste. However, there is a difference between an acceptable level of toxic accumulation and a level that leads to ill health. Toxins can be formed by the faulty digestion of protein and fat, which can occur when the liver is not functioning optimally. You can stimulate digestion by eating the right foods for your body type, which will promote proper protein and fat breakdown. The recipes in this book are specifically designed to increase enzyme release that aid good digestion, as well as facilitate the elimination of waste products from the body.

Elimination of harmful toxins will leave you feeling great and bursting with energy, giving a healthy glow to your skin, hair, teeth, and nails. If you frequently have no energy or less energy than you used to have, and your skin is broken out and your hair dull, or you are constantly getting colds, flu, headaches, and allergies, you probably need to detox. A lot of the health problems that we suffer from are due to excessive use or abuse of foods, drink, drugs, and pollutants. In large quantities these become toxic to the body, clogging the tissues and suffocating the cells. The result is a decrease in energy and a weaker immune system.

The way we live today provides lots of opportunities for overindulgence in social situations, for example, at dinner parties, at nightclubs with friends, and at your favorite bar. An excess of alcohol, nicotine, coffee, tea, candy, chocolate, sugar, too many fatty foods, and social drugs often starts as a social habit and soon turns into a regular pastime. If we overindulge in these things, we can never feel healthy all the time.

All ancient cultures have traditionally practiced detoxification processes as an important part of their lifestyle. The practices outlined in this book provide a solid foundation with which to continue this tradition into our lives today. All the recipes hold to the principle that what we eat should not only be nutritious and healthy but should also help to promote detoxification and cleansing by stimulating and toning the body's channels of elimination via the skin, kidneys, bowels, and lungs.

HOW DO I DETOX AND NOT FEEL MISERABLE?
The first step to improving your health and beginning your detox is to cut out the habits that cause toxins. If you find this difficult, even cutting down or taking a week's break would be of great benefit. This will help to cleanse the body and enhance the elimination of toxins.

Some people do experience side effects or reactions such as cold sores, acne, and headaches when toxins are reduced or released. To support this process, drink plenty of water and take lots of exercise and multivitamin supplements. If the reaction is too uncomfortable or an illness such as a skin condition gets progressively worse, consult a health care professional.

The second step is to start replacing bad habits with ones that promote good health. Exercise regularly, especially when stressed, drink lots of water instead of coffee or tea, and snack on fruits and juices—you'll be surprised at how tasty a good juice is!

Most of our recipes avoid dairy and wheat products where possible as these are the two most common triggers for allergies and intolerances in people's diets. But we know that you'll find our recipes as delicious and naughty-feeling as the foods you are used to eating, and the best bit about it all is that you'll feel great after eating them. In fact, if we hadn't told you they were from a detox menu, you would probably have felt guilty for eating them!

WHAT IS TRADITIONAL CHINESE MEDICINE (TCM)?

TCM talks about the fundamental aspects in all healthy beings as the harmonious balance between opposing yet interrelated principles. These principles, often labeled yin and yang, represent the duality of nature that combine to make it a whole.

The familiar yin/yang diagram represents the duality of life. The yin darkness slowly turns into the yang light and the yang lightness slowly turns into the yin dark. In the yin phenomenon there is a little yang and in the yang, a little yin. The yang label represents the active, masculine, thermally *hot* quality of all things in life. The yin represents its passive, feminine or *cold* quality.

To understand one aspect of the pair you need to consider its opposite. Thus, night exists in relation to day to create time; left is relative to right to signify direction; up to down to represent height; and hot to cold to represent temperature.

HOT AND COLD BODY TYPES

The yin/yang phenomenon relates to body type in the form of the body's thermal nature. The yang or Hot qualities that apply to our personality and constitution are, for example, being prone to having a warm body and dry skin; an outgoing personality and a loud voice; a red complexion; a focused, logical mentality and a more aggressive, masculine manner. Conversely, the yin or Cold qualities are a cooler body and moist skin; a pale complexion; an introverted personality; a serene, intuitive mentality and a more timid and passive, feminine manner.

The terms "masculine" and "feminine" do not denote sexual gender but are aspects within all of us. Most people fluctuate between these two aspects. Fundamentally though, one is constitutionally more yin than yang or vice versa.

THE THERMAL NATURE OF FOOD

Just as people have a certain thermal nature, so does food. The effect of food on the body once it has been digested has a certain energetic property, which may cause a change in body temperature. Thus we can talk about "warming" or "cooling" foods. There are also foods classified as neither warming or cooling which are "neutral."

Cooling foods direct energy inwards and downwards, primarily cooling the upper and outer parts of the body. Warming foods move energy upwards and outwards from the center of the body to its extremities. Warm foods are said to speed us up and cool foods are said to slow us down.

WARMING FOODS
- *Vegetables:* carrots, leeks, onions, shallots, scallions, watercress
- *Fruit:* apricot, blackberry, blackcurrant, cherry, mango, strawberry, peach, quince
- *Grains, dried seeds, legumes:* oats, lentils, quinoa
- *Seeds and nuts:* pumpkin, sesame, sunflower and watermelon seeds, chestnuts, walnuts
- *Herbs and spices:* basil, bay leaf, caraway seeds, cardamom, chives, cinnamon, cloves, coriander leaves (cilantro) and coriander seeds, cumin, dill, fennel seeds, fenugreek, garlic, ginger, lemongrass, mustard, nutmeg, oregano, pepper, spearmint, star anise

COOLING FOODS

- *Vegetables:* broccoli, cauliflower, zucchini, corn, asparagus, white mushrooms, radishes, lettuce, cucumber, celery, Swiss chard, eggplant, spinach, summer squash, cabbage, bok choi
- *Fruit:* watermelon, apple, tomato, all citrus fruits, persimmons, cantaloupe, banana, pear, coconut, pineapple
- *Grains, dried seeds, legumes:* soy milk, soybean sprouts, tofu, tempe, mung beans and their sprouts, alfalfa sprouts, barley, millet, wheat and wheat products, amaranth
- *Herbs and spices:* peppermint tea, dandelion tea, nettle tea, lemon balm tea, white peppercorns, marjoram, tarragon, turmeric
- *Others:* kelp and seaweed, wheat grass, spirulina, barley grass, yogurt, crabmeat, clams

NEUTRAL FOODS

- *Vegetables:* beets, Brussels sprouts, fennel, parsnips, pumpkin, pole beans, snow peas, squash, rutabaga, sweet potato, taro, turnip, yam
- *Fruit:* date, fig, grape, guava, papaya, plum, raspberry
- *Grains, dried seeds, legumes:* brown rice, rye, corn, aduki beans, navy beans, peas, red kidney beans
- *Seeds and nuts:* almonds, peanuts (fresh in shells), pine nuts, raisins
- *Herbs and spices:* parsley, rosemary, sage, thyme

OTHER TYPES OF DETOX

There is a wide range of detox diets available, many of which promote very little choice of food. They range from one to three-day fasts, to months at a time. We recommend that some of these fasts should not be done while working as they are not conducive to normal life and often leave people feeling exhausted. Detoxes based on Chinese principles do not advocate food deprivation as it depletes energy in the stomach and spleen. The following list shows examples of fasting detoxes, but we recommend that you do not follow any of them solely on the basis of the information given here.

1. A diet of fresh fruit and vegetables and whole grains only, with lots of water to drink. Most people find this diet one of the easier of the strict detoxes to follow.

2. A diet of brown rice only, with lots of liquids such as water and herbal/green teas. People do this fast for a couple of weeks and often feel very weak. Side effects such as headaches are common.

3. A diet of purely fruit and vegetables. This helps to cleanse the digestive tract but can be difficult to stick to for any length of time and people following it say they have no energy.

4. Liquid cleanses or fasts. Juices, vegetable broths, and teas are used to purify the body while fasting. Again, tiredness is a common side effect of this type of fast and it is not recommended that you undertake it while continuing any normal activities, such as working.

5. Water fasting is more intense than juice fasting and often results in the person feeling lethargic and lacking energy.

QUICK REFERENCE TIPS FOR HEALTHY EATING

- Choose organic produce and eat whole food with lots of fiber
- Reduce refined foods such as sugar, fatty foods, additives, and colorings
- Don't drink a lot of liquid with your meals as this dilutes the digestive juices
- Chew food thoroughly
- Eat in a relaxed environment and never eat while upset or during an argument
- Eat small regular meals and don't overeat
- Drink adequate water and herbal teas daily (see water consumption opposite)
- Moderate or eliminate stimulants or drugs such as alcohol, caffeine, and nicotine
- Exercise regularly

WATER CONSUMPTION

The kidneys filter large volumes of waste from the body each day. Basically, they are a highly sensitive mechanism of pumps that function to regulate fluid balance, blood pressure and excrete metabolic toxins. Fluid intake requirements are different for each of us according to our body. With too much water, the kidneys lose their subtle function to gauge how much water the body needs. It has been a popular practice to drink at least 2$^1/_2$ quarts (8 glasses) of water each day. According to the principles of Chinese medicine, this practice will deplete the proper functioning of the kidneys to regulate fluid levels in the body. The solution calls for a level of intuition regarding how much water to consume each day. There are, however, certain key factors to remember. First and most obviously, drink according to your thirst. Second, it is more helpful for proper digestion to drink outside of meal times; at least 30 minutes to an hour before and after food intake. Third, when drinking any fluid it is important to take small amounts at any time, rather than guzzling down a whole cup in one swig.

Once again the proper functioning of the kidneys is based on recognizing subtle changes in the body's fluid level. If the kidneys are overburdened with sudden bursts of water over a short period of time, their responsiveness will be less effective. You can vary the amount of water you need according to your amount of physical activity. However, hot body types generally require more water consumption than cold body types. The way to gauge exactly how much to drink is that if you begin to feel uncharacteristically more cold after water consumption, drink less. If you don't drink much water and you feel excessively hot, drink regularly but moderately to abate the feeling.

DETERMINING YOUR BODY TYPE

In order to use this book optimally you need to determine your thermal nature. In doing so you can begin to balance your diet suited to your body type, and detox effectively and safely. Below are two questionnaires to determine your body type and thereby point you in the direction of the foods and recipes which will be most effective for you.

ARE YOU A HOT PERSON?

	yes	no	sometimes
1. Do you often feel hot?	☐	☐	☐
2. Do you have a red or ruddy complexion?	☐	☐	☐
3. Are you often restless, impatient, excitable, or hyper?	☐	☐	☐
4. Do you talk fast and walk fast?	☐	☐	☐
5 Do you suffer from dry eyes, skin, or throat?	☐	☐	☐
6. Do you have problems sleeping or getting off to sleep?	☐	☐	☐
7. Are you prone to red eyes?	☐	☐	☐
8. Are you prone to headaches?	☐	☐	☐
9. Are you always thirsty, especially for cold drinks?	☐	☐	☐
10. Do you fidget a lot?	☐	☐	☐
11. Do you have a rapid heart rate?	☐	☐	☐
12. Are you prone to sudden changes in your health?	☐	☐	☐
13. Do you have dark, scanty urine?	☐	☐	☐
14. Do you throw off the bed covers at night?	☐	☐	☐
15. Do you like to lie stretched out in bed?	☐	☐	☐
16. Are your arms and legs and body hot to the touch?	☐	☐	☐
17. Do you have a loud voice?	☐	☐	☐
18. Do you like to talk a lot?	☐	☐	☐
19. Is your breathing heavy and loud?	☐	☐	☐
20. Do you have skin problems (e.g., eczema, psoriasis)?	☐	☐	☐
Totals	☐	☐	☐

ARE YOU A COLD PERSON?

	yes	no	sometimes
1. Do you feel the cold?	☐	☐	☐
2. Are you a quiet person?	☐	☐	☐
3. Do you walk slowly and talk slowly?	☐	☐	☐
4. Are you prone to edema or water retention?	☐	☐	☐
5. Do you urinate often and/or with pale watery urine?	☐	☐	☐
6. Are you often tired, sleepy, or listless?	☐	☐	☐
7. Are you prone to watery eyes and/or nose?	☐	☐	☐
8. Do you have a slow heart rate?	☐	☐	☐
9. Does your health change gradually?	☐	☐	☐
10. Do you like to be covered up in bed?	☐	☐	☐
11. Do you like to curl up in bed?	☐	☐	☐
12. Do your arms, legs, and body feel cold to the touch?	☐	☐	☐
13. Do you prefer hot drinks?	☐	☐	☐
14. Do you have a weak or quiet voice?	☐	☐	☐
15. Do you dislike talking?	☐	☐	☐
16. Do you rarely have a thirst?	☐	☐	☐
17. Are you relaxed and easy going?	☐	☐	☐
18. Are you vulnerable to colds?	☐	☐	☐
19. Do you have shallow or weak breathing?	☐	☐	☐
20. Do you prefer not to be very active?	☐	☐	☐
Totals	☐	☐	☐

Fill out both questionnaires and add up the total for each column. If you answer mostly "YES" to the questions in "Are you a hot person?" then you should choose cooling recipes or neutral recipes. If you answer mostly "YES" to the questions in "Are you a cold person?" you should choose warming recipes or neutral recipes.

If you answer mostly "SOMETIMES" in both questionnaires, you are a neutral person. You can therefore have a wide variety of recipes from all the sections.

warming foods

warming foods
for cold people

Without heat, life slows down and we become cold and sluggish. Cold people dislike the cold, love the heat and are often overdressed and attracted to warm foods and drinks. Too much cold in the body can be due to many factors such as:

- **lack of physical activity**
- **eating too many cooling foods (see page 8) and/or not enough warming foods**
- **over-exposure to an extremely cold climate**
- **constitutional weakness at birth**

If you are a cold person, avoid foods that will make you feel even colder. Eat more warming foods and fewer raw and cooling foods. When you do eat cooling foods, boil, bake, pressure-cook or deep-fry to make them warmer. Don't eat food below room temperature and avoid putting ice in drinks. See page 8 for a full list of warming foods.

When warming foods are eaten, they push the blood and energy from deep inside to rise up and out to the surface of the body. If we heat ourselves up too much so that we sweat, we will lose energy when we cool down. To avoid this, balance warming foods with those from the neutral section, as they will not make you any colder. Remember that it takes longer for a cold person to create warmth than it does for a hot person to cool down. Chewing food thoroughly also creates more warmth, so a cooling food chewed thoroughly can become more warming.

SPICY ROOT SOUP

This soup is a great detoxifier, as it helps the liver, the lymphatic system, the bowel, urinary, and nervous systems. Parsnips have medicinal value, and simple Chinese remedies still use them to treat coughs, colds, rheumatism, and arthritis. Serves 2

1 tablespoon olive oil **1 large onion, finely chopped**	Gently fry in a pot over low heat for 2–3 minutes, until the onion starts to soften.
1 garlic clove, crushed **$^1/_2$ teaspoon ground coriander** **$^1/_4$ teaspoon ground cinnamon** **$^1/_2$ teaspoon ground cumin** **$^1/_4$ teaspoon ground ginger** **3 cardamom pods** **Pinch of chili powder or 2 teaspoons curry powder** **1 bay leaf**	Add to the pot and fry for another 2 minutes, until the spices start to release their aromas.
$^1/_2$ lb (about 2 $^1/_2$ cups) parsnips, peeled and diced **1$^1/_2$ cups celery root, peeled and diced** **1$^1/_4$ cups vegetable stock**	Add to the pan, cover, and simmer for 20 minutes until the vegetables are soft.
2$^1/_2$ cups vegetable stock	Add and simmer for another 10 minutes.
Salt and freshly ground black pepper **Fresh cilantro, for garnishing**	Season to taste and serve garnished.

CARROT, ORANGE, AND GINGER SOUP

These ingredients are beneficial if you have a hangover or feel as if you are beginning to get a cold. The orange in this soup is an excellent source of water-soluble vitamin C. Ginger helps to push out a cold or fever and is good for relieving the discomfort of diarrhea, stomach gas, and gout. Serves 2

1 medium onion, finely chopped, **3 medium carrots, peeled and finely sliced** **1½ cups water**	Place in a large pot, bring to a boil, and simmer for 15 minutes, until the carrots are soft.
2 inches ginger root, peeled and finely grated	Gather all the bits into your hand and squeeze the juice into the soup. Discard the ginger fiber.
1½ cups water **Zest of ½ orange** **Juice of 1 orange** **Pinch of sea salt or Kosher salt** **Freshly ground black pepper**	Add to the pot, bring back to a boil, and simmer for another 10 minutes.
Chopped chives, for garnishing	Add to the pot, then remove from the heat. Purée in a food processor or blender until smooth. Reheat and serve garnished.

PUMPKIN, PORCINI, AND FRESH DILL SOUP

The pumpkin in this soup helps the spleen, stomach, and kidneys. Its nutrients are known to calm a hyperactive fetus, so this is a good soup to eat during the last trimester of pregnancy. Dill is a stimulant for the liver's detoxing function. It helps to prevent stomach gas and the accumulation of food residue in the intestines. Serves 2

³/₄ **ounce porcini mushrooms** ²/₃ **cup boiling water**	Place in a bowl and let soak.
1 onion, chopped **1 garlic clove** ¹/₂ **cup vegetable stock**	Cook over low heat in a pot, covered, until the onion is soft, about 10 minutes.
¹/₂ **cup fresh mushrooms, sliced** ¹/₂ **lb. pumpkin, peeled, seeded, and diced** ¹/₄ **teaspoon dried thyme** **1 teaspoon dried sage** **Pinch of grated nutmeg** **2 teaspoons soy sauce** **1 cup vegetable stock**	Add to the pot, cover, and simmer for 10 minutes, or until the pumpkin is tender.
	Drain the porcini mushrooms, reserving the water, and add them to the pot. Pour the water through a strainer with a paper towel to remove any grit.
Freshly ground black pepper **1 tablespoon fresh dill weed, chopped** **1 cup vegetable stock**	Add to the soup along with the porcini liquid, and simmer for 5 minutes. This soup may be served as it is or blended for a creamy texture.

warming foods

MISO AND GINGER SOUP

Miso is rich, yet subtle in flavor and extremely good for you. It is made from soybeans, which can lower the risk of heart disease. It also reduces menopausal symptoms and is thought to help prevent cancer. Together with ginger, this soup aids digestion, helps prevent nausea, and is good for sweating out a cold.
Serves 2

½ **cup vegetable stock**	Heat in a pot.
2 medium onions, sliced into half moons	Add to the pot. Cover and simmer for 5 minutes.
1 garlic clove, crushed	
2 tablespoons very thinly sliced ginger	
1½ teaspoons dried sage	
2 tablespoons brown miso	Add to the pot. Cover and simmer for 20 minutes or until the vegetables are soft. Serve immediately.
1 carrot, sliced in rounds	
3½ cups vegetable stock	

TOM KA KAI

The chicken in this soup is an energy tonic. It helps the kidneys, spleen, and stomach because it is good for digestion, poor appetite, and diarrhea. It also builds up the blood, making it good for palpitations and anemia. Coconut milk is a complete protein food that strengthens the body, so is very good to drink during convalescence. Serves 4

3½ cups (28 oz.) coconut milk **2 cups (16 oz.) chicken stock**	Bring to a boil in a large pot.
1 small red chili, left whole but pricked with a knife **4 stems lemongrass** **1 inch galangal, or ginger root** **¼ teaspoon ground black pepper** **6 kaffir lime leaves**	Add to the pot and simmer for 20 minutes.
1 chicken breast, boned, skinned, and cut into strips **4 oz. (about 1 cup) shiitake or white mushrooms**	Add to the pot and simmer for another 10 minutes or until the chicken is cooked yet tender. Remove the spices with a slotted spoon.
2 scallions, chopped **¼ cup lime juice** **Pinch of sea salt or Kosher salt, optional** **Fresh cilantro, for garnishing**	Add, and serve garnished with cilantro.

RAW YANG PURITY

In a balanced diet, it is important to alternate the consumption of raw foods with the consumption of cooked foods. The warming vegetables and herbal ingredients in this all-raw dish will help to circulate blood around the body, give support, and comfort the detoxing organs.

cilantro
mustard greens
onion
parsley
kale
leeks
parsnip
pepper
scallions
celeriac
watercress

There are no strict measurements as the idea is that you can make a very quick and simple salad using whatever you have available in your fridge, and that the quantities can be varied to give a different taste each time you make it.

This is the essence of detox, and this recipe should become a staple, being eaten as a snack and/or with meals.

It is best made using a meat grinder, but a food processor will do. Wash the vegetables and roughly chop them. Grind them in the meat grinder or blend them in the food processor until everything is chopped very finely. Scoop into a bowl and serve. You may squeeze some fresh lemon juice over the salad to prevent it turning brown if you like. It will keep in the fridge for no more than a day.

ADUKI* AND KIDNEY BEANS WITH CREAMED AVOCADO DRESSING

Aduki beans detoxify by removing swelling and water accumulation in the lower region of the body. They also tone up the heart and spleen by promoting the flow of fluids. Avocado contains fourteen minerals that regulate the body's functions and stimulate the growth of skin, hair, teeth, and nails. Its copper and iron content aids red blood regeneration and improves energy levels. Serves 2

FOR THE DRESSING

1 avocado, pitted and peeled
juice of 1/2 lemon
2 tablespoons water
1/2 teaspoon paprika
Dash of tabasco sauce
Pinch of salt

Place in a blender or food processor and purée to a smooth creamy texture.

7-8 oz. can of kidney beans, (about 1 cup) drained and rinsed
7-8oz. can of aduki beans, drained and rinsed
1 stalk celery, chopped
1 apple, chopped
1 scallion, chopped
4 cherry tomatoes, cut in half
5 basil leaves, torn into pieces
1 handful chopped chives

Place in a salad bowl, mix together well, and pour the dressing over it. Toss well and serve.

*Also called adzuki and azuki beans

CYPRIOT SALAD

Haloumi is a tasty salty cheese made from sheep's milk. It doesn't have the allergic effects of cow's milk cheese because the size of its protein particles enables better digestion. Serves 2

2 ounce piece of haloumi cheese, cut into ¼-inch slices, then diced

Toast under a medium broiler on a nonstick baking sheet until golden brown. Turn once and brown the other side.

4 medium tomatoes
¼ cucumber, sliced
¼ yellow pepper, cored, seeded, and diced
1 handful of flat-leaf parsley, roughly chopped
10 black olives, pitted
½ red onion, thinly sliced
3–4 large lettuce leaves, torn into pieces

Mix with the cheese in a salad bowl.

FOR THE DRESSING
2 tablespoons extra-virgin olive oil
1 tablespoon white wine vinegar
1–2 teaspoons lemon juice
Pinch of sea salt or Kosher salt
Freshly ground black pepper

Mix well and pour over the salad. Toss well.

VALENCIANA

Rice strengthens the spleen and pancreas by expelling toxins from the body. It is a tropical grain that is thought to soothe people who get irritable when the weather is very hot. The Chinese feed rice to those with a poor appetite and weak digestion. It is also given to nursing mothers who have painful, swollen breasts. Serves 2

a generous ½ cup brown rice	Place in a pot with plenty of water and boil until tender (about 30 minutes). Drain and let cool, then transfer to a salad bowl.
2 scallions, chopped **1 tablespoon pine nuts, toasted until golden** **5 cherry tomatoes, cut in half** **8 black olives, pitted and cut in half** **1 small handful raisins** **1 tablespoon chopped parsley** **2 teaspoons tomato paste** **1 teaspoon soy sauce** **1 teaspoon vinegar**	Add to the rice, mix well, and serve.

ROAST PEPPER AND BASIL DIP

This protective dish uses sweet peppers, which contain vitamin A, vitamin B complex, and C. There is as much vitamin C in peppers as there is in oranges, making them good for building up resistance to colds and flu. Basil is a warming energy-giving herb that induces sweating and harmonizes the stomach, to aid gentle digestion. Serves 2

Preheat the oven to 400°F.

1 large red pepper

Roast on a baking tray in the oven for 20–30 minutes, or until the skin goes black. Remove from the oven and let cool. Peel off the skin, and seed and core, saving any juice.

¹/₂ cup soy milk
¹/₂ teaspoon paprika
¹/₂ teaspoon salt
2 teaspoons extra-virgin olive oil
2 teaspoons cider vinegar
1 tablespoon chopped basil

Place in a blender or food processor with the pepper flesh and juice, and purée to a smooth creamy texture.

Serve chilled as a dip or warm as a sauce for other dishes.

SALADS and SNACKS

BEET, ARUGULA, APPLE, AND CASHEW NUT SALAD

This is a powerful, mineral-rich meal. The high iron content in the beets helps to purify the blood and promote menstruation. It also strengthens the heart and sedates the spirit. Cashews are a good source of magnesium, helping to reduce incidence of osteoarthritis. Apples cleanse the body and protect against disease-producing bacteria in the stomach. Serves 2

1 large or 2 small fresh beets, peeled and finely chopped
1 dessert apple, finely chopped
2 large handfuls fresh arugula, washed and chopped

Place in a salad bowl.

¼ cup cashews, chopped

Place on a baking sheet under the broiler on medium heat, and toast until golden brown. Turn once or twice to brown all sides.

1 carrot, peeled

With a vegetable peeler, cut thick shavings of carrot. Add to the bowl with the cashew nuts and mix well.

FOR THE DRESSING
2 teaspoons extra-virgin olive oil
2 tablespoons fresh lemon juice
Pinch of sea salt or Kosher salt
Freshly ground black pepper

Mix the dressing and pour it over the salad immediately before serving.

TERRINE OF FENNEL, BRAZIL NUT, AND SAGE

Sage is a highly antiseptic and rejuvenating herb that can help fight off infection. It improves the immune system, stimulates digestion, and eases liver complaints. Ancient Greeks called sage the "immortal herb" and the Egyptians praised it as a lifesaver, hence its botanical name *Salvia*, meaning to save. Serves 2

Preheat the oven to 375°F.

6 ounces Brazil nuts (about 1½ cups)

Place on a baking tray and roast in the oven for 10 minutes until golden brown. Let cool, then place them in a blender or food processor and purée until they are finely chopped.

1 teaspoon extra-virgin olive oil
1 fennel bulb, finely chopped
1 small onion, finely chopped
½ teaspoon fennel seeds

Place in a pan, covered, and cook over low heat for 6–7 minutes.

7–8 white mushrooms, finely chopped
1 tablespoon sage leaves or 1 teaspoon dried

Add to the pan, cover, and cook over low heat for another 5 minutes, until the mushrooms start to release their juices.

Freshly ground black pepper
1 tablespoon soy sauce

Add to the nut and vegetable mixture and blend to a rough paste.

Scoop into a small greased loaf pan, press down evenly, and cover with a piece of wax paper to prevent it drying out. Bake for 20 minutes.

This dish goes well with a simple tomato sauce, such as the sauce for lima bean and coriander potato cakes (see page 73).

MARINATED SHRIMP WITH RED PEPPER AND TOASTED SESAME SEEDS

Some Chinese studies show that sesame lowers blood sugar levels. Research has also shown that garlic can be used as a treatment for numerous health problems including gastritis, dysentery, and constipation. Ginger rids the body of toxins, aids digestion, and helps soothe nausea. Serves 2

1¹/₂ cups cooked shrimp
1 small garlic clove, crushed
¹/₂-inch piece ginger root, peeled and grated
¹/₂ teaspoon garam masala
¹/₄ teaspoon turmeric
¹/₄ red chili, seeded, and finely chopped
4 teaspoons lemon juice

Mix in a bowl and let marinate for 1 hour.

¹/₂ red pepper, cored, seeded, and thinly sliced
1 scallion, chopped
1 small handful of fresh bean sprouts
2 teaspoons sesame seeds, toasted

Add to the bowl, mix well, and serve immediately. A rice salad or other grain dish would complement this salad.

STEAMED CITRUS MUSSELS

Mussels strengthen the liver and kidneys and are an important remedy for raising the body's energy levels. They also help regulate menstruation and stimulate the process of semen production. Serves 2

1 garlic clove, crushed **¹/₂-inch piece ginger root, peeled and finely sliced** **2 stems fresh lemongrass, outer leaves removed, and finely chopped** **¹/₄ cup rice wine vinegar or white wine vinegar** **¹/₄ cup dry white wine (optional) or water** **Juice of ¹/₂ lemon**	Place in a large pot, bring to a boil, and simmer for 5 minutes.
2 pounds fresh mussels, well scrubbed	Add to the pot, cover with a lid, and cook over low heat for 3–4 minutes, shaking the pot occasionally.
¹/₃ cup coconut milk **Juice of 1 lime**	Add when the mussels are open, and cover and shake once or twice to coat all the mussels in the sauce. Discard any mussels which have not opened, and serve immediately.

RED DRAGON PIE

Potatoes are anti-viral, anti-inflammatory, and can help digestion. Recent research has found that they contain certain properties that may be effective against cancer. The antioxidant quality of the skin helps a variety of degenerative diseases. Ancient Chinese people believed that potatoes could even relieve the toxic symptoms of chicken pox. Serves 2

Preheat the oven to 400°F.

¾ cup aduki beans, soaked for 8 hours and drained	Boil in plenty of water for 10 minutes, then reduce the heat and simmer for 40 minutes or until tender.
1 large potato, diced	Boil until tender and drain.
1 teaspoon sesame seeds **2 teaspoons soy milk**	Add to the potatoes and mash together.
1 teaspoon extra-virgin olive oil **1 medium onion, finely chopped**	Place in a pan and fry gently, covered, for 5 minutes, until the onion is softened.
½ red pepper, cored, seeded, and cut into strips **½ green pepper, cored, seeded, and cut into strips** **1 teaspoon paprika**	Add to the pan and fry, covered, for another 5 minutes.

½ **teaspoon dried basil**	Add to the pan, bring to a boil, then simmer very gently for 15 minutes.
2 tablespoons tomato paste	
4 teaspoons brown miso	
2 teaspoons soy sauce	
²/₃ **cup water**	
	When the beans are cooked, drain and add to the sauce, stirring them in well. Scoop into an ovenproof dish, and top with the mashed potatoes. Bake in the oven for 25 minutes, until bubbling and browned on top.

BAKED MUSHROOMS STUFFED WITH OLIVES AND WALNUTS

Mushrooms contain germanium, which increases oxygen efficiency in the body, counteracts the effects of pollutants, and increases resistance to disease. They are also a good source of vitamin B complex. Olives quench thirst and promote the flow of body fluids. Serves 2

	Preheat the oven to 375°F.
4 large flat mushrooms	Remove the stalks and set aside.
²/₃ **cup olives**	Place in a blender or food processor, along with the mushroom stalks. Blend until all the nuts are broken down and the mixture is quite paste-like.
1 cup walnuts	
1 tablespoon chopped parsley	
	Divide the mixture among the mushrooms, and push evenly into each cavity. Place on a nonstick baking sheet and bake in the oven for 20–25 minutes, until the mushroom flesh is succulent and cooked. Serve hot.

GINGER, ADUKI BEAN, AND CELERY ROOT CAKES

Ginger sweats out colds and flu. It can also speed up blood circulation and aids digestion to create feelings of general well-being. Celery root is packed full of useful nutrients that are effective for maintaining the lymphatic system and preventing the onset of arthritic ailments. Serves 2

14 ounces celery root, peeled and cut into cubes (about 3½ cups) **½ pound potato, peeled and cut into cubes (about 1¾ cups)**	Boil until tender, drain, and reserve.
2 teaspoons extra-virgin olive oil **1 small onion, finely chopped**	Gently fry for 5 minutes, until the onion is soft.
½ teaspoon ground coriander **½ teaspoon ground cumin** **½ teaspoon paprika** **½ teaspoon ground cinnamon** **1 teaspoon dried thyme**	Add to the pan and cook for another 5 minutes.
2 teaspoons soy sauce **14-oz. can aduki beans, drained and rinsed**	Place in a bowl along with the potatoes and celery root, add the onion mixture, and mash well together.
1 tablespoon all-purpose flour **1 tablespoon extra-virgin olive oil**	Form into burgers and coat with a little flour. Oil a heavy-based frying pan and cook over medium heat. Fry the burgers until they are golden brown, then turn and cook the other side.

ROASTED PUMPKIN STUFFED WITH MUSHROOM AND GARLIC

The antiseptic and antioxidant action of garlic cleanses the liver and drives away infection. Pumpkins are high in potassium and sodium, and are a good source of vitamins B and C. They benefit the spleen and stomach, and stabilize a hyperactive fetus. Serves 2

Preheat the oven to 400°F.

1 small pumpkin

Slice the top off and scoop out the seeds, reserving the top.

1 teaspoon extra-virgin olive oil
1 small onion, finely chopped

Place in a small pan and fry gently, covered, for 5–6 minutes, until the onion is softened.

2 garlic cloves, crushed
1 teaspoon dried mixed herbs
½ teaspoon black mustard seeds

Add to the pan and fry for 1 minute, until the mustard seeds start to pop.

5 ounces white mushrooms,
** finely chopped (about 1½ cups)**

Add to the pan, cover, and cook over low heat for 5–10 minutes until done.

Pinch of sea salt or Kosher salt

Season, then fill the pumpkin with the mushroom mixture and replace the top. Stand the pumpkin in a small ovenproof dish, supported with toothpicks, if necessary. Bake in the oven for 50–60 minutes, until the flesh is soft.

To serve, remove the top and slice into halves or quarters.

ANDEAN QUINOA AND VEGETABLE STEW

Quinoa is a high-protein cereal that strengthens the energizing functions of the whole body. It also contains even more calcium than milk and is a very good source of iron and vitamin B complex and vitamin E. Serves 2

¼ cup brazil nuts, broken in half	Roast or broil for 5–10 minutes until golden, then set aside.
5 ounces quinoa (about ¾ cup) **1¼ cups water**	Place in a pot, bring to a boil, and simmer for 10–15 minutes until tender; strain and set aside.
1 tablespoon extra-virgin olive oil **1 medium onion, finely chopped**	Gently fry in a covered pot for 5–6 minutes, until the onion is softened.
1 teaspoon ground cumin **1 teaspoon ground coriander** **1 red chili, seeded and finely chopped**	Add to the pot and fry for another minute.
1 celery stalk, finely chopped **1 carrot, sliced** **1 medium potato, diced** **½ red pepper, cored, seeded, and cut into strips** **1 tablespoon water**	Add to the pot. Cover and cook over low heat for 5–10 minutes.
14-oz. can chopped tomatoes **1 teaspoon dried oregano** **Pinch of sea salt or Kosher salt**	Add, cover, and simmer gently for another 10 minutes, until the stew is thickened.
	Add the nuts and quinoa to the stew and simmer very gently for 3–4 minutes until well mixed and evenly heated. Serve immediately.

PEACH AND MANGO CRUMBLE

A yummy dessert that is also good for detoxing —is that possible? Peaches benefit the stomach and large intestine channels. They promote blood circulation and the flow of body fluids, thereby moistening dryness and remedying constipation. The sweet and sour qualities of mangoes quench thirst. They settle the stomach and encourage digestion. Serves 2

Preheat the oven to 375°F.

1 peach, quartered
1 mango, peeled, and cut into chunks
1 cup unsweetened apple juice

Place in a pan and simmer very gently for 15 minutes until the fruit is tender and the juice has reduced and thickened. Transfer to an ovenproof dish.

³/₄ cup oats
2 tablespoons soy margarine
2 teaspoons honey
2 teaspoons sesame seeds
¹/₄ cup chopped almonds

Mix together with your fingers until the oats are coated with the fat and honey.

Spread the oat crumble topping over the fruit and bake in the oven for 20 minutes until golden brown.

Serve hot with cashew cream (see page 80).

YANG FRUIT COMPOTE

This stewed fruit concoction contains minerals, vitamins, enzymes, and fiber, making it easily digestible and cleansing. Cherries are often used to improve the blood and to treat anemia. Cinnamon is a potent antiseptic that warms the whole system. In summer, it can be served as a simple fruit salad. Serves 2

10 blackberries
10 cherries
4 dried figs, chopped
1 peach, pitted and chopped
2 apricots, pitted and chopped
$1/4$ teaspoon ground cinnamon
2 tablespoons apple juice

Place in a pan and simmer very gently for 20 minutes, until the juices are released and the fruit is tender. Serve warm.

SPICED BROWN RICE PUDDING

Brown rice is full of B vitamins and is therefore excellent for the nervous system, helping to relieve depression. Rice soothes the stomach, strengthens the spleen and pancreas, increases energy, and expels toxins. Rice pudding is very therapeutic; the longer it is cooked, the more therapeutic it becomes. Serves 2

Preheat the oven to 350°F.

2¹/₂ cups water

Bring to a boil in a large pot.

a scant cup short-grain brown rice

Add and simmer for 15 minutes. The rice should be half-cooked. Strain, and return to the pot.

1¹/₄ cups soy milk
2 tablespoons rice syrup or date syrup
¹/₂ teaspoon ground cinnamon
¹/₈ nutmeg, grated
2 whole cloves
1 small handful of raisins
2 shavings of orange peel

Add to the pot and bring to a boil, then simmer very gently for 20 minutes.

Soy milk (if needed)

Scoop the rice into a very lightly greased ovenproof dish, cover with a lid or foil, and bake in the center of the oven for 40 minutes, until the rice is very tender. Add more soy milk if the rice begins to look dry.

Serve with chopped fruit such as bananas or mangoes.

FRESH FRUIT CAKE

Oats contain B vitamins, making them an excellent body-builder. Their soothing quality allows them to strengthen the stomach and spleen and tone up the chi. Oats are a natural agent which are high in fiber, and because they can be digested quickly, they pass easily into the colon and help to destroy the putrefactive poisons caused by the decomposition of other foods. Serves 2

Preheat the oven to 350°F.

2¹/₂ cups chopped fresh fruit, such   Mix all together in a large bowl.
   as peaches, blackberries, raspberries,
   dates, cherries, or plums
2 generous cups oats
a scant 2 cups all-purpose flour
1¹/₃ cups dry, unsweetened coconut
1 cup sunflower oil
1¹/₂ cups unsweetened fruit
   juice
1¹/₂ tablespoons date syrup
a generous ¹/₂ cup raisins

Scoop into a 9-inch nonstick cake pan. Bake in the oven for 45 minutes, until brown and firm to the touch. Cool on a wire rack.

HOT FIGS IN A GINGER AND PLUM SAUCE

In Chinese medicine, figs are known as "bright vision fruit" because the carotene in them helps our ability to see in dim light. They are also great energy providers and are eaten as a stomach tonic. Plums are good for the liver and stomach because they promote the production of digestive fluids. Serves 2

6–7 red plums, cut in half, pitted, and sliced

2 tablespoons rice syrup or maple syrup

¹/₂ teaspoon ground ginger

Heat in a pan, stirring to prevent it from burning.

Juice of ¹/₂ lemon

As the plums begin to soften and liquefy, add the lemon juice and bring to a boil. Cook for a few minutes, stirring continuously, until the sauce thickens.

Push the sauce through a fine strainer, to remove any pieces of plum skin. Return to the pan and keep warm over a very low heat.

6 fresh or canned figs

2 tablespoons apple juice

Heat in a pan and cover until the apple juice comes to a boil. Reduce the heat and simmer very gently for 2–3 minutes to heat the figs through; they do not need to be cooked.

Arrange the figs on serving plates and pour the sauce over them. Serve hot, with a little cashew cream (see page 80).

warming foods

WARMING MUESLI

Seeds are a high protein food, containing more protein than grains. They are concentrated sources of vitamins B complex, D, and E, the minerals calcium, magnesium, iron, and zinc. This makes them an ideal energy and vitality-enriching food.

6 parts oats

1 part linseeds

1 part dry, unsweetened coconut

1 part pine nuts

$\frac{1}{2}$ part walnuts

1 part sunflower seeds

3 parts dried dates, chopped

You can make up as much muesli in advance as you wish, and keep it in an airtight container.

blackberries

cherries

soy milk

Serve with soy milk, topped with the fresh fruit. Soak the muesli in the soy milk for 10–20 minutes before serving.

CARROT, APPLE, AND GINGER JUICE

The antioxidant quality of carrot and ginger makes this a great anti-aging juice. It is also a great remedy for the onset of a cold or flu and for nausea, morning, and travel sickness. Carrot cleanses the digestive tract and detoxifies the liver. Apples contain pectin, which binds to toxic metals such as mercury and lead, and carries them out of the body. Serves 1

3–4 large carrots
2 dessert apples
Piece of ginger ¹/₂-inch x ¹/₂-inch

Take the tops off the carrots and quarter the apples, there is no need to peel anything.

Push all ingredients through a juicing machine, serve immediately.

APPLE, CINNAMON, AND CLOVE JUICE

This is great to drink when you feel a cold coming on, or simply feel under the weather. Cinnamon warms the whole system and cloves have natural antiseptic qualities. Serves 1

3 dessert apples

Quarter and push through the juicing machine.
Warm the apple juice gently in a pan, without boiling.

4 cloves

Add to juice in pan, then pour juice into tall glass.

¹/₂ teaspoon ground cinnamon

Add to juice in glass and serve immediately.

neutral foods

neutral foods

If a person is not clearly hot or cold, then a diet balanced in warming, cooling, and neutral properties is best. As a neutral person you can eat all the delicious recipes from all the sections to try and remain as balanced as possible. See page 8 for a list of neutral foods. As a hot or cold person you can eat recipes from this section as well as recipes from the appropriate section for your body type.

TOMATO BISQUE

Tomatoes help to clear heat, and are great thirst-quenchers. Bell peppers are a good source of beta-carotene, iron, and potassium, which protect and build a strong immune system. Parsley contains more vitamin C than many citrus fruits, helping the body to defend itself against harmful bacteria. Serves 2

8 large fresh tomatoes, roughly chopped	Blend in a blender or food processor, and set aside.
1 teaspoon extra-virgin olive oil **1 small onion, finely chopped**	Place in a large pot, cover, and cook over low heat for 10 minutes, until the onions are golden.
2 teaspoons tomato paste	Add to the onions along with the pulped tomatoes, bring to a boil, and simmer for 10 minutes uncovered.
2¹/₂ cups vegetable stock **2 teaspoons soy sauce**	Add to the pot and simmer for 10 minutes.
1 tablespoon chopped basil **Juice of ¹/₂ lemon**	Add to the pot, simmer for another 2 minutes, and serve.

LENTIL AND CARROT SOUP

This easily digestible no-fuss soup provides a rich mineral supply to the whole body. Lentils are high in magnesium, potassium, phosphorous, and manganese—all extremely beneficial for the proper functioning of the muscular and nervous systems. Carrots expel toxins from the bladder and bowels. They are also useful for liver and kidney problems. Serves 2

1 teaspoon extra-virgin olive oil	Place in a large pot and cook over low heat gently, covered, for 5 minutes,
1 medium onion, finely chopped	until the onions are soft.
1 stalk celery, finely chopped	
1 large carrot, peeled and sliced	Add to the pot, cover, and cook over low heat gently for another 10
2 tomatoes, skinned and chopped	minutes, until the carrot starts to soften.
1 small garlic clove, crushed	
1 bay leaf	
1 teaspoon ground coriander	
$^1/_2$ teaspoon ground cumin	
$^3/_4$ cup puy lentils, soaked for 12 hours and drained	Add to the pot and bring to a boil. Simmer, covered, for about 1 hour, until the lentils are very tender.
3 cups vegetable stock or water	
1 tablespoon soy sauce	Add to the pot when the lentils are tender.
Chopped parsley, for garnishing	Serve garnished.

SOUPS

SPICED GAZPACHO

Tomatoes are used to treat anorexia and acts as a liver stimulant to help eliminate toxins. They are rich in beta-carotene and lycopene, two anti-cancer nutrients, and together with the chili, this soup cleanses the lungs. Cultures that use chilies in their diets have a low incidence of respiratory problems. Serves 2

½ small cucumber
1 lb. good-quality fresh
    tomatoes
½ red onion
½ yellow pepper, cored and seeded
1 garlic clove, crushed
1 red chili, seeded, and finely
    chopped
1 small handful of parsley
1 small handful of cilantro
2 teaspoons extra-virgin olive oil
Pinch of sea salt or Kosher salt
Pinch of paprika
Freshly ground black pepper
1 tablespoon cider vinegar

Place all ingredients in a food processor and blend until they are well chopped, but not puréed.

Parsley and cilantro, for
    garnishing

Serve at room temperature, garnished.

CHESTNUT, CHICKPEA, AND DILL SOUP

Of all nuts, chestnuts are the lowest in fat. Their sweetness complements the delicate flavor of aromatic spices like dill, which has a cleansing effect on the liver. In small amounts, dill stimulates the energy of the body and removes stagnant energy. It also has a very calming effect on digestion and on the mind.

Serves 2

1⅓ cups dried chickpeas, soaked overnight, then drained and rinsed 5 cups water Pinch of sea salt or Kosher salt 1 stalk celery, chopped 1 leek, sliced 2 bay leaves 1 tablespoon fresh dill or 1 teaspoon dried dill 2 teaspoons soy sauce	Place in a large pot, bring to a boil, and simmer uncovered for 1½ hours until the chickpeas are very tender and the liquid has reduced by half.
1 tablespoon extra-virgin olive oil 2 garlic cloves, crushed	Heat the oil in a pan and gently fry the garlic for 2–3 minutes until golden.
14-ounce can whole chestnuts ½ teaspoon paprika	Add to the garlic. Mash together and cook gently for 5 minutes. Remove bay leaves and dill from the chickpeas, add the chestnut mixture, and stir well. This soup may be served as it is or blended for a creamy texture.

LIMA BEAN, RED PEPPER AND CILANTRO SOUP

Lima beans need to be cooked in an uncovered pot to let gas escape from them. They contain lots of trace minerals, and minerals like potassium, magnesium, and zinc, which are beneficial for the muscular system. Serves 2

Preheat oven to 375°F.

½ red pepper, cored and seeded, cut lengthwise

Place cut-side down on a baking tray and roast in the oven or under a broiler on medium-high heat. When the skin has blackened and the flesh is soft, remove from the heat and let cool. Peel off the skin and set aside.

2 teaspoons extra-virgin olive oil
Pinch of Hungarian paprika
1 small onion, finely chopped

Place in a large pot and gently fry for 10 minutes, until the onion is very soft. Add the roasted red pepper and continue to gently fry for another 3–4 minutes.

14-ounce can lima beans, drained and rinsed
1 tablespoon finely chopped cilantro
3 cups water

Add to the pot. Bring to a boil, and gently simmer for 10 minutes.

Pinch of black pepper
Pinch of sea salt or Kosher salt
2 cilantro leaves, for garnishing

Season, then purée in a blender or food processor until smooth. Serve garnished.

BEET AND ORANGE SOUP

This soup combines the nutritional and immune-stimulating properties of an orange, with the blood-cleansing effects of beets. Recent studies have shown specific anti-carcinogenic substances in beets—so this is more than a soup, it's also a powerful tonic. Serves 2

1 teaspoon extra-virgin olive oil **1 small onion, finely chopped**	Fry gently in a large pot, covered, for 10 minutes, until the onion is soft.
a generous cup raw beets, peeled and cut into 1-inch pieces **1 small potato, peeled and diced**	Add to the pot, cover, and cook over low heat gently for another 5 minutes.
3 cups vegetable stock	Add and bring to a boil. Simmer, covered, for 25–30 minutes until the vegetables are soft.
Zest of ½ orange **Juice of 1 orange**	Add to the pot and simmer for 2–3 minutes. Remove from the heat and let cool for a few minutes.
	Purée the soup in a blender or food processor until smooth. It may be difficult to get the beets really smooth, but don't worry—it adds a little texture.
Pinch of sea salt or Kosher salt **Freshly ground black pepper**	Season to taste, return to the pot, and reheat to serve.

neutral foods

RAW GREEN PURITY

Chlorophyll is the pigment that gives all plants their green color. It is an effective detoxifier because it protects against toxic chemicals and inhibits the growth of germs and bacteria. Like chlorophyll, alfalfa helps guard against disease. It is a therapeutic food that contains all the known vitamins and minerals necessary for life. Alfalfa detoxifies the liver by neutralizing harmful acids, thereby purifying the blood and aiding digestion. It combines with the other ingredients to make a salad that has an antioxidant, anti-inflammatory effect. It is extremely rich in amino acids, organic acids, minerals, and trace minerals.

alfalfa sprouts
beets
cabbage
carrots
Napa cabbage
kohlrabi
green beans
turnip
grapes
(a very small amount of onion or leeks may be used for flavor)

There are no strict measurements as the idea is that you can make a very quick and simple salad using whatever you have available in your fridge, and that the quantities can be varied to give a different taste each time you make it.

This is the essence of detox, and this recipe should become a staple, being eaten as a snack and/or with meals.

It is best made using a meat grinder, but a food processor will do. Wash the vegetables and roughly chop them. Grind them in the meat grinder, or put them in the food processor and blend until everything is chopped very finely. Scoop into a bowl and serve. You may squeeze some fresh lemon juice over the salad to prevent it from turning brown, if you like. It will keep in the fridge for no more than a day.

SHIITAKE MUSHROOM RICE SALAD

The shiitake mushroom is a powerful stimulant for the immune system—large quantities can actually increase the body's resistance to disease. It can be used to treat a whole range of symptoms including high cholesterol levels, hypertension, and colds. Serves 2

³⁄₄ cup brown rice **¹⁄₄ teaspoon saffron**	Place in a pan with enough water to cover and boil for 30 minutes, or until tender. Drain and let cool, then transfer to a salad bowl.
1 sheet nori seaweed	Toast over a flame or under the broiler for a few seconds, until the color changes. Tear into pieces and add to the rice.
2 ounces shiitake mushrooms, sliced (about ¹⁄₂ cup) **1 tablespoon chopped parsley**	Add to the rice.
2 teaspoons soy sauce **Juice of ¹⁄₂ orange**	Mix together in a small bowl.
1-inch piece ginger root, grated	Gather up all the pieces in your hand and firmly squeeze the juice into the soy and orange mixture. Pour this over the salad and mix well. Serve with a selection of other salads.

GUJERATI CARROT SALAD

Carrots contain large amounts of vitamins, minerals, and enzymes that help to lower blood pressure, prevent infection, and maintain the health of almost every organ in the body. Cilantro and scallions calm digestion and detoxify the blood. Serves 2

3 carrots, peeled and grated **2 scallions, finely sliced** **1 tablespoon chopped cilantro**	Place in a bowl.
1 teaspoon black mustard seeds	Heat a dry frying pan over a medium flame, add the seeds, and dry-roast them until they begin to pop. Add to the bowl.
2 teaspoons dry, unsweetened coconut	Dry-roast in the same way, until it turns golden brown and releases its aroma. Add to the bowl.
Pinch of sea salt or Kosher salt **Juice of ½ lemon (or more to taste)**	Add and mix thoroughly. Serve chilled.

SHRIMP, POTATO, AND BASIL SALAD

The Chinese believe that the energy creatures possess when alive can be transferred to the eater, so shrimp is an excellent choice for those who suffer from lethargy and lack drive. Potatoes draw out the toxins that the over-consumption of meat produces. Serves 2

1 pound new potatoes, diced	Boil until tender, drain, and let cool.
2 tablespoons basil leaves, torn **4-6 radishes, sliced** **1 scallion, chopped**	Place in a bowl with the potatoes and mix well.

neutral foods

½ **pound peeled shrimp (about 1¾ cups)**	Gently mix in.
Juice of ½ lime ½ **cup unflavored yogurt** **Freshly ground black pepper**	Mix together and pour over salad.
A few lettuce leaves, for serving	Arrange on a plate and place the shrimp salad on top.

LOBIO (KIDNEY BEAN AND WALNUT SALAD)

When using nuts, buy them fresh in their shells. Commercially shelled nuts are generally chemically treated to process them out of their shells and to preserve them. Walnuts are rich in protein and fatty acids that eliminate impurities from the intestines and nourish the nervous system. Kidney beans are a high-protein food that repair and build tissue. They improve the body's metabolism and cleanse the digestive tract.

Serves 2

14-ounce can red kidney beans, drained and rinsed or 1 cup dried beans, soaked and boiled	Place in a bowl.
$1/2$ stalk celery, chopped	
1 tablespoon chopped scallion	
1 tablespoon chopped cilantro	
1 tablespoon diced yellow pepper	
FOR THE DRESSING	
1 garlic clove	Blend together until the mixture is a paste.
$3/4$ cup shelled walnuts	
1 tablespoon wine vinegar	
$1/4$ cup water	
1 $1/2$ tablespoons walnut or extra-virgin olive oil	Add slowly, and blend until the dressing is smooth. Pour the dressing over the salad and mix well.
Pinch of sea salt or Kosher salt	
Freshly ground black pepper	
Pinch of cayenne pepper	
1 tablespoon chopped cilantro, for garnishing	Garnish and serve.

ASPARAGUS, SMOKED SALMON, AND DILL SALAD

The warm and bitter quality of asparagus promotes urination, which is why it is often advised for kidney problems. It also cleanses the arteries of cholesterol, soothes broken out skin, and promotes blood circulation. Oily fish is a rich source of omega-3 essential fatty acids—nutrients that improve blood cholesterol levels and reduce inflammation of the joints, skin, and other body tissues. Serves 2

8 asparagus spears	Trim off the hard woody ends. Steam or boil the spears until they are just tender, then drain. Place under a medium broiler until they are just beginning to brown, then let cool.
2–3 leaves sweet romaine lettuce	Arrange on a serving dish.
2 ounces smoked salmon (lox), cut in thin strips	Build a lattice with the asparagus by putting 2 spears one way and the next two at 90° and so on, using all 8 spears.
2 teaspoons roughly chopped dill **4–5 green olives**	Arrange over the lattice.
2 teaspoons lemon juice **2 teaspoons extra-virgin olive oil**	Mix together and pour over the salad.
Freshly ground black pepper	Sprinkle over the salad and serve.

BELGIAN ENDIVE, WATERCRESS, AND SEVILLE ORANGE

Bitter foods such as Belgian endive stimulate the release of enzymes that settle the stomach and have a favorable effect on digestion. Watercress helps to break down kidney and bladder stones and is good for the health of the skin. Oranges stimulate movement of the bowels, and act as an internal antiseptic agent.

Serves 2

2 heads Belgian endive	Slice the Belgian endive, place in a salad bowl, and squeeze the lemon
Juice of ½ lemon	juice over it to stop it turning brown.

1 bunch of watercress, stalks removed and roughly chopped	Add to the bowl and toss well.
2 Seville oranges, peeled, sliced, and quartered	
1 carrot, grated	
⅓ cup apple juice	
Freshly ground black pepper	

BEAN SPROUTS WITH BELL PEPPERS AND RED CABBAGE

Bell peppers are a rich source of vitamin C. They help to improve digestion and circulation in the body. Bean sprouts contain enzymes that stimulate the body's cleansing and healing processes. They flush toxins from the body and help to destroy cancer cells. Red cabbage also improves digestion, beautifies the skin, and proves useful as an ulcer remedy. Serves 2

2 handfuls mixed bean sprouts	Combine in a salad bowl and serve.
½ red pepper, cored, seeded, and cut into thin strips	
½ green pepper, cored, seeded, and cut into thin strips	
¼ small red cabbage, finely sliced	
Juice of 1 sweet orange	

COUSCOUS MAGHREB

Couscous is made from durum wheat semolina. It stimulates the liver to cleanse itself of toxins. Apricots contain large amounts of antioxidants which also help to eliminate toxins from the body. Chickpeas contain high levels of iron and are a good source of unsaturated fatty acids. Serves 2

2 teaspoons extra-virgin olive oil **1 small onion, finely chopped**	Cook over low heat in a large pot, for 5 minutes, until the onion starts to soften.
1 garlic clove, crushed **1 teaspoon apple spice or pumpkin pie spice** **1 teaspoon ground coriander**	Add to the pot and cook over low heat for another 5 minutes.
1 zucchini, cut in 1/2-inch slices **14-ounce can chickpeas, drained and rinsed** **14-ounce can chopped tomatoes** **5 dried apricots, roughly chopped**	Add to the pot and simmer for 10–15 minutes, until the apricots begin to swell up.
1 1/4 cups vegetable stock	Add to the pot and bring to a boil.
1/3 cup couscous	Add to the pot and stir well. Cover, and lower the heat. Cook for 4–5 minutes, until the couscous has puffed up and is tender.

BROILED LEMON SOLE

Lemon sole is a temperate-water white fish that provides a superior form of protein to other types of fish. It also contains minerals such as iodine that are hard to find in other foods. Basil is an aromatic, digestion-enhancing herb. It has an antiseptic effect that makes it a good treatment for nausea and dysentery.

Serves 2

Preheat the oven to 375°F.

6 cherry tomatoes
½ cup fennel, sliced
2 teaspoons extra-virgin olive oil

Arrange in a small ovenproof dish, then bake for 15 minutes until tender.

2 double fillets of lemon sole,
   6 ounces each
2 sprigs of tarragon, bruised

Place the fillets on a baking tray, skin-side up. Divide the tomatoes and fennel between the fillets, arranging them on the wider end. Place one sprig of tarragon on each, then carefully fold the fish over to form a roll. Secure with a toothpick.

Pinch of sea salt or Kosher salt
Freshly ground black pepper

Season, then cook under a medium-hot broiler until the fish begins to brown, then carefully turn to cook both sides.

2 wedges of lemon, for garnishing
1 teaspoon chopped tarragon, for
   garnishing

Garnish and serve with salad or steamed vegetables.

neutral foods

DOUBLE-BAKED SWEET POTATOES

Sweet potatoes are one of the most nutritious vegetables and are especially useful for eliminating harmful heavy metals like mercury, lead, cadmium and copper. These toxins can remain in the body for a long time and cause problems with the body's metabolic system unless they are removed. Serves 2

	Preheat the oven to 375°F.
2 large sweet potatoes	Bake whole for 40–50 minutes until soft.
1 teaspoon extra-virgin olive oil **1 small onion, finely chopped**	Gently fry for 5 minutes.
½ teaspoon ground cumin **½ teaspoon ground coriander** **4–5 white mushrooms, chopped**	Add to the pan and fry for another 5 minutes.
Dash of soy sauce, to taste **1 teaspoon dried oregano**	Add to the pan and remove from the heat.
	Cut each sweet potato in half lengthwise and gently scoop out the flesh, being careful not to tear the skin. Add the flesh to the onion mixture and mix together well, adding more soy sauce if you like.
Sesame seeds	Place the potato skins on a nonstick baking tray and fill with the onion mixture. Sprinkle with a few sesame seeds. Bake in the oven for 20 minutes, then serve immediately.

CRISPY CORN FRITTERS

This recipe is a fun and easy way to enjoy the nutritious value of corn. It is rich in vitamins A, C, E, and B-complex vitamins. Its vitamin B3 content stimulates circulation and reduces cholesterol levels in the blood. Soy flour from soybeans is high in calcium and contains complete protein. It has very little saturated fat and is a good source of lecithin, an essential fatty acid which can reduce inflammation and aid metabolism. Serves 2

2 tablespoons soy or gram flour **1 tablespoon cornmeal** **1/4 cup water**	Mix together in a bowl with a whisk.
1/2 teaspoon baking soda **1/2 teaspoon salt** **1 teaspoon ground coriander** **1/2 teaspoon ground cumin**	Add to the bowl and mix well.
7-ounce can corn, **rinsed and drained** **1 tablespoon chopped cilantro**	Add to the bowl and stir in.
1 tablespoon sunflower oil	Heat in a heavy frying pan. Spoon in the batter—there should be enough for 4 fritters. Fry over medium heat for 3–4 minutes until crisp and golden brown, then turn and cook the other side. Serve with a pungent salad such as the marinated shrimp (page 33).

LIMA BEAN AND CORIANDER POTATO CAKES

Lima beans are highly alkalizing. They neutralize acidic conditions brought about by the overconsumption of meat and refined foods, making them important for the health of the liver, lungs, and skin. Serves 2

1¼ pounds potatoes, diced	Boil until tender, strain and reserve.
2 teaspoons extra-virgin olive oil **1 small onion, finely chopped** **½ teaspoon ground black pepper** **½ teaspoon ground coriander**	Gently fry for 4–5 minutes until the onions are soft but not brown.
14-ounce can lima beans, **drained and rinsed** **½ teaspoon salt** **2 tablespoons chopped cilantro**	Place in a bowl with the potatoes and onion and mash together. Form the mixture into cakes.
1 tablespoon extra-virgin olive oil	Heat in a heavy nonstick pan and fry the cakes in batches to avoid overcrowding the pan. Cook for 3–4 minutes on each side until crisp and golden.
FOR THE SAUCE **2 teaspoons extra-virgin olive oil** **1 small onion, finely chopped**	Fry in a pan for 4–5 minutes until soft.
14-ounce can chopped tomatoes **1 teaspoon dried basil** **2 teaspoons soy sauce** **Freshly ground black pepper** **1 teaspoon cider vinegar**	Add to the pan and simmer for 20 minutes, stirring occasionally until reduced to a thick consistency.
	Serve 2 cakes per portion and top with the sauce.

FRESH BEAN CASSOULET WITH GARLIC POLENTA WEDGES

Fresh beans are useful for treating the symptoms of diabetes. Polenta is a by-product of corn, which is one of the most balanced starches that helps to prevent cancer and lowers the risk of heart disease.

Serves 2

2 teaspoons extra-virgin olive oil **1 onion, finely chopped** **1 clove garlic, crushed**	Cook over low heat in a covered pot for 10–15 minutes until the onion is soft but not brown.
1 carrot, sliced **¹/₄ cup fennel, roughly chopped** **³/₄ cup mushrooms, sliced** **3 sprigs rosemary** **1 bay leaf** **1 sprig thyme**	Add to the pot and cook over low heat for another 6–7 minutes, until the mushrooms release their juices.

14-ounce can cannellini beans, drained and rinsed	Add to the pot and bring to a boil. Simmer for 15–20 minutes.
³/₄ cup fava beans	
³/₄ cup Italian green beans or flat beans, sliced diagonally	
1¹/₄ cups vegetable stock	
2 teaspoons soy sauce	Add to the pot and simmer for about 5 minutes to thicken the sauce.
Freshly ground black pepper	
1 heaping teaspoon cornstarch or potato flour, mixed with a little cold water	

FOR THE GARLIC POLENTA WEDGES

1¹/₂ cups water or vegetable stock	Bring to a boil in a large pot.
¹/₂ cup polenta or cornmeal	Add slowly, stirring continuously.
Pinch of sea salt or Kosher salt	Add when the mixture starts to thicken. Continue to stir until the mixture resembles a smooth porridge, 4–5 minutes.
Freshly ground black pepper	
1 clove garlic, crushed	
¹/₂ teaspoon dried mixed herbs	

Scoop the polenta into a 9-inch round, nonstick, baking pan, smooth the surface, and let cool. It will solidify. Once it is cool, cut the polenta into wedges. Transfer the wedges to a large baking sheet and broil until crisped brown. Serve hot with the cassoulet.

TOMATOES STUFFED WITH CHESTNUTS, VIETNAMESE-STYLE

This recipe combines the cooling nature of tomatoes with the warming effect of chestnuts. Tomatoes help to purify the blood and aid in digestive problems, such as indigestion and constipation, to improve appetite. Chestnuts promote reproductive capacity and protect against premature aging. Serves 2

Preheat the oven to 375°F.

4 large tomatoes

Slice off tops with a sharp knife. Scoop out centers with a spoon, being careful not to cut the skin of the tomato, or it will split when baked. Reserve the tops and centers of the tomatoes and put the tomato shells to one side.

1 teaspoon extra-virgin olive oil
¹/₂ medium onion, finely chopped
2 garlic cloves, crushed

Fry gently for 10–15 minutes until the onion is soft and golden.

14-ounce can whole chestnuts,
**   drained and rinsed**

Add to onions and mash to a lumpy paste with the back of a fork. Take the pan off the heat.

1 small handful of cilantro,
**   chopped**
Juice and grated rind of ¹/₂ lemon
Pinch of salt
Freshly ground black pepper

Add to chestnut mixture and stir well.

Stuff the chestnut mixture carefully into the tomato shells using a spoon.

FOR THE SAUCE

1 teaspoon extra-virgin olive oil
½ medium onion, finely chopped
1 mild red chili, seeded and very
   finely chopped

Fry for 10–15 minutes until onion is soft and golden.

1 large tomato, chopped

Chop, and add to pan along with reserved tomato flesh and tops.

Pinch of sea salt or Kosher salt
Freshly ground black pepper

Season, then simmer uncovered for 10 minutes, until the sauce is thick. Blend the tomato mixture in a food processor.

Pour the sauce into an ovenproof dish large enough for the stuffed tomatoes to fit into snugly. Sit the tomatoes on top of the sauce and bake for 30 minutes, until the tops start to brown and the tomatoes are soft. Serve with rice.

BELL PEPPER AND CASHEW NUT FLAN

Bell peppers regulate blood pressure and improve circulation through the body. They contain large quantities of vitamins A, B complex, and C, and are good for general health. The high levels of zinc, magnesium, iron, and folic acid in cashew nuts function as a laxative and activate the enzymes that control energy levels. Serves 4

Preheat the oven to 375°F.

1 red pepper **1 yellow pepper**	Roast in the preheated oven for 20–25 minutes, or until the skins begin to turn black. Remove and place in a bowl covered with plastic wrap until cool. Peel off the skins and remove the cores and seeds.
1 portion oaty pastry dough (see page 97)	Use to line a 12-inch tart pan or quiche dish.
1 medium onion, sliced	Spread in the pie shell with the roasted peppers and set aside.
7 ounces cashew nuts (1³/₄ cups)	Grind in a blender or food processor until they are quite fine.
¹/₂ pound spinach leaf, washed **1¹/₂ cups soy milk** **¹/₂ teaspoon black pepper** **1 teaspoon whole-grain mustard** **¹/₂ teaspoon paprika** **¹/₄ teaspoon grated nutmeg** **1 teaspoon salt**	Add, and blend until the spinach is finely chopped.
7 ounces extra-virgin olive oil (a scant cup) **1 tablespoon cider vinegar**	Slowly add the oil and then the vinegar.
Paprika	Pour the cashew mixture over the peppers and onions, sprinkle with paprika, and bake in the oven for 25 minutes, until the top has slightly browned and the flan is quite firm to touch. Serve hot or cold.

CASHEW NUT CREAM

Cashews are a great source of magnesium, a nutrient that aids the functions of heart tissue and also stimulates the production of calcium, which aids bone development and growth. Cashews are high in protein and essential omega-6 fatty acids that prevent heart disease and maintain healthy cells. Use in place of cream. Serves 2

1 cup cashews
¹/₂ cup soy milk

Place in a blender and purée until creamy.

1 teaspoon honey
¹/₂ cup sunflower oil
1 teaspoon lemon juice

Add the honey, then slowly pour in the oil—you will see the mixture thicken—then finally add the lemon juice to set the cream.

MANDARIN CHEESECAKE

This cheesecake contains tofu, which has four times more protein than milk and twice as much calcium. It contains nutrients that replenish the blood and strengthen the muscles and bones. Besides being extremely low in fat, tofu is also a good source of protein and minerals. Serves 2

9 ounces low-fat, low-sugar oat cookies

Place in a food processor and blend until fine.

⅓ cup soy margarine

Melt in a pan, then add to the cookies and blend briefly. Press the mixture into a 10-inch tart pan or quiche dish and refrigerate for 20 minutes to set.

1¼ pounds soft tofu
1 teaspoon vanilla extract

Place in a blender or food processor, and purée until smooth.

2 tablespoons concentrated apple juice or rice syrup
⅛ teaspoon powdered agar agar

Heat the liquid in a pan and add the agar agar. Bring to a gentle simmer, stirring continuously until the grainy texture of the agar agar disappears. Add to the tofu and blend together. Pour immediately over the cookie base and spread evenly. Refrigerate for 15 minutes to set.

½ pound all fruit (no sugar or sweetener) marmalade

Heat in a pan until melted and pour evenly over the cheesecake.

2 fresh mandarin oranges, peeled and divided into segments

Arrange on top and leave until cooled and set.

SPICED BAKED BANANAS WITH HONEY AND YOGURT

Bananas help to counteract toxins in the body. They are a source of potassium—an important mineral that helps to lower cholesterol and maintain blood pressure levels. Yogurt is also beneficial for health as it provides "friendly" bacteria that help to protect the intestinal tract. Serves 2

Preheat the oven to 400°F.

2 large bananas, peeled and sliced lengthwise
1 teaspoon soy margarine

Place the bananas in a very lightly greased ovenproof dish and spread the rest of the margarine on each slice.

1 tablespoon fresh orange juice
Pinch of ground cinnamon
Pinch of ground cloves
1 cardamom pod
2 teaspoons honey

Mix together and pour over the bananas. Cover with a lid or foil and bake in the oven for 20 minutes, until the bananas are soft.

1¹/₂ tablespoons unflavored low-fat yogurt

Serve hot with a spoonful each.

MIXED BERRY CORN MUFFINS

The berries in this recipe are high in vitamins A and C, and contain calcium, magnesium, and iron. Their fiber content stimulates digestion, and eliminates waste from the body. Rice flour contains B vitamins that are beneficial for the nervous system. Makes 10 large or 15 small muffins.

Preheat the oven to 400°F.

2¼ cups rice flour
a generous cup polenta or cornmeal
1 ½ teaspoons baking soda
2 tablespoons soft brown sugar

Sift into a bowl.

1⅓ cups fresh or frozen mixed berries, such as cranberries, blueberries, blackberries, redcurrants or blackcurrants
1 dessert apple, cored, peeled, and grated

Add to the bowl and mix together.

¾ cup yogurt
2 tablespoons lemon juice
1 tablespoon sunflower oil
⅔ cup unsweetened apple juice

Mix together, then pour into the bowl and stir it in to make a soft batter. You may need a little extra apple juice. It should easily spoon into a non-stick muffin pan, putting 1 spoonful into each case. You should have enough for 10–15 muffins.

Bake in the oven for 15 minutes, or until golden. Let cool, then transfer to a wire rack. These muffins freeze well.

APPLE AND CINNAMON CAKE

Cinnamon combined with the energy of apples encourages the body's lymphatic system to work more efficiently, thereby promoting proper circulation. It has a cleansing action due to its antiseptic, aromatic, and astringent qualities. Serves 2

Preheat the oven to 375°F.

¹/₃ cup soy margarine
1 large tablespoon rice syrup

Cream together in a large bowl.

1 large Granny Smith apple, peeled and grated

Mix into the bowl.

1¹/₂ cups whole-wheat flour
1 tablespoon soy flour
1 tablespoon wheat germ
¹/₂ teaspoon baking soda
2 teaspoons ground cinnamon

Sift into the bowl and mix together well.

¹/₄ cup raisins
2 tablespoons soy milk
Juice of ¹/₂ lemon

Add to the bowl and mix until you have the consistency of a very thick batter, adding more soy milk if necessary.

Scoop the mixture into a nonstick 9-inch cake pan lined with wax paper. Bake in the oven for 30–40 minutes, or until the cake springs back to the touch.

Let cool, then tip out onto a wire cooling rack.

ORANGE OAT CAKE

The iodine in oats makes them useful for eliminating harmful toxins from the body. This mineral helps to regulate the body's metabolism and weight. Oats help to lower blood pressure, high cholesterol, and blood sugar levels. They are a rich source of vitamin B complex, so they protect the nervous system of people under stress. Serves 2

Preheat the oven to 375°F.

1 cup whole-wheat flour
1 heaping tablespoon soy flour
2 teaspoons baking powder
1 teaspoon grated nutmeg
2¹/₂ cups medium oatmeal, or
   oats blended to a flour
¹/₂ cup wheat germ

Mix together in a large bowl.

2 large tablespoons date syrup or
   rice syrup
¹/₂ cup soy milk
¹/₃ cup water
¹/₄ cup sunflower oil
Zest and juice of 1¹/₂ sweet oranges
1 heaping teaspoon sugar-free
   marmalade

Mix together, then pour into the bowl and beat together to form a fairly firm consistency.

Scoop into a 9-inch nonstick cake pan lined with wax paper. Bake in the oven for 35–40 minutes, until firm and golden. Leave in the pan for 5–10 minutes, then tip out on a cooling rack.

DESSERTS and DRINKS

CITRUS DREAM

The combination of vitamin C and honey provides a quick-fix cure for the symptoms of colds, flu, and coughs. This juice can also be enjoyed when you are in perfect health! Serves 1

½ **cup freshly squeezed**
    orange juice
½ **cup pineapple juice**
1½ **tablespoons honey**
8 ice cubes
Juice of ½ **lemon**

Place in a blender, purée well, and serve immediately.

CLEANSING: CARROT, CUCUMBER, AND SPINACH JUICE

This juice is strongly detoxifying and is very calming for the digestion. Aloe vera is non-toxic and has powerful healing qualities that help to alleviate ulcers and gastrointestinal disease. It is also reputed to have anti-cancer properties. Wild blue-green algae has been described as a "superfood" because of its great harmonizing effects on body and mind. It contains practically every known nutrient; it builds the blood, acts as a liver stimulant, and can relieve depression. Serves 1

4 carrots
quarter of a large cucumber
1 small handful fresh spinach leaves

Wash the vegetables well, and push them through a juicing machine (be careful not to use too much spinach as the flavor can be very strong).

$^1/_2$ teaspoon aloe vera
$^1/_2$ teaspoon wild blue-green algae

Add the aloe vera and blue green algae supplements, stir very well, and serve.

PURITY: BEET, CELERY, APPLE, AND CARROT JUICE

This classic blend of vegetables and apple contains beta-carotene, which helps to cleanse the skin. It works by stimulating the growth and regeneration of skin cells while helping to protect against the development of cancer cells. The juice has other benefits, too. If you suffer from digestive problems, you will find this a soothing remedy. It also lowers high blood pressure and calms rheumatic pains. Serves 1

$^1/_2$ large beet, raw
2 stalks celery
2 apples
4 carrots

Push through a juicing machine and serve in a chilled glass.

DESSERTS and DRINKS

BARLEY WATER

Barley water is a very alkalizing and efficient blood cleanser that can be helpful in the treatment of cystitis. It can help build the stomach and spleen, making it useful for indigestion and general stomach pain. Drink this juice for an energy boost, as it is also a fatigue-reliever. Serves 1

Take 1 cup of whole barley and soak overnight in water. If you can't manage to soak the barley overnight, soak it for at least an hour before boiling the grain. Cook the grain in 3 cups of water until the grain is soft. Discard the grain and strain the water into a container, then let it cool. Add lemon juice and honey to taste (avoid honey if there are symptoms of candidasis present). Store in the refrigerator for up to a week. Drink half a glass every morning, preferably on an empty stomach.

FLATBREAD

This bread is an excellent way of enjoying grains and is an ideal accompaniment to any meal. It is preferable to eat complex carbohydrates with other grains and legumes, rather than with animal meat. Makes 6

a generous ¹/₂ cup whole-wheat flour
a generous ¹/₂ cup all-purpose flour

Place in a bowl.

¹/₃-¹/₂ cup water

Add very slowly until you can form a soft dough (if you add too much, simply flour your hands and mix until a soft dough forms). Knead the dough for 5–6 minutes, shape into a ball, cover with a damp cloth, and leave for 20 minutes.

Form the dough into 6 small balls and keep covered with the damp cloth. Heat a heavy frying pan over medium-low heat without oil; this will take a few minutes.

Optional:
1 teaspoon sesame seed
1 teaspoon black mustard seeds

Take a ball and flatten it onto a lightly floured surface. Dust with flour—and sesame or mustard seeds, if desired—and roll it out thinly and evenly into a 5–6 inch circle. Place in the hot pan and cook for 1–2 minutes, until bubbles begin to form. Turn over and cook the other side for 30–60 seconds. Keep warm on a plate covered by a clean dish towel. Repeat with the other balls and serve immediately.

CARAWAY RYE BREAD

Rye has a very low calorific value, which makes it popular with people watching their weight. Caraway encourages digestion of the nutrients in rye. It also strengthens and tones the stomach. This bread freezes well. Makes 2 small loaves.

Preheat oven to 400°F.

4 cups rye flour
2³/₄ cups rice flour
1 teaspoon salt

Sift into a large bowl.

2 packets fast-action or
    quick-rise dried yeast

Mix into the bowl.

1¹/₄ cups apple juice
1¹/₄ cups hot water

2 tablespoons honey
1 tablespoon caraway seeds

Mix until liquid is at blood heat. Make a well in the flour, add the liquid, and stir into the flour.

Water

Add and mix until it forms a dough. Transfer to a floured surface and knead well for 10 minutes. Divide into 2 equal portions and place in 2 small nonstick loaf pans, or shape into loaves and place on a nonstick baking sheet. Gently cover with clean dish towels and leave in a warm place until the loaves have doubled in size.

Caraway seeds

Sprinkle over the tops of the loaves. Bake in the oven for 45 minutes, or until risen and the loaves sound hollow when knocked on the bottom. Let cool for a little before tipping onto wire cooling racks.

MALTED SUNFLOWER OAT BREAD

Sunflower seeds are said to be a perfect food. They tone the chi, which means they provide a lot of energy for the body. They contain high levels of polyunsaturated fatty acids and help to remove toxins from the body. Oats help to soothe and restore the nervous and reproductive systems and are low in fat.

Makes 2 small loaves

	Preheat the oven to 350°F.
5 cups old fashioned oats	Place in a food processor and blend to a fine flour.
one package fast-action or quick-rise dried yeast **2 tablespoons sunflower seeds** **1 teaspoon salt**	Place in a large bowl with the oat flour.
2 tablespoons malt extract **1³/₄ cups warm water** **1 tablespoon sunflower oil**	Mix together, make a well in the flour, and pour in the liquid. Mix together and then form into a dough.
	Knead the dough for 10 minutes until it is elastic, then divide into 2 portions and place in 2 small, nonstick, loaf pans. Cover with a clean cloth and leave in a warm place for 30 minutes until the dough has slightly risen.
	Bake in the oven for 50–60 minutes until the bread is browned and risen, and it sounds hollow when tapped on the bottom. Tip out onto a wire rack and leave until cooled.

SIMPLE SODA BREAD

This is a yeast-free bread that is ideal for people with candidasis—the overgrowth of candida (yeast-like fungi) in the body. Makes 1 large loaf

Preheat the oven to 400°F.

4 cups whole-wheat flour
2 cups white bread flour
1½ teaspoons baking soda
2 teaspoons baking powder
Pinch of sea salt or Kosher salt

Mix together in a large bowl.

2 cups plain low-fat yogurt
 mixed with ⅔ cup water
1 teaspoon honey

Make a well in the center and pour in gradually. Stir to mix, and then knead gently to form a dough, soft and moist, but not sticky. Do not knead too much, just enough to form an even dough.

Shape the dough into a round loaf on a greased baking sheet, and score a cross in the top. Bake in the oven for 40–50 minutes, until browned, or until it sounds hollow when tapped on the bottom. Let it cool on a wire rack, covered with a clean cloth.

For best taste and texture, eat while still warm.

VEGAN CRÉPES

Vegan diets do not contain any animal products, including eggs and dairy produce—the two most common allergies in people's diets. This recipe for pancakes is a very healthy alternative. Makes 4 crépes

½ cup self-rising flour **Pinch of sea salt or Kosher salt** **Pinch of ground black pepper**	Place in a bowl.
⅔ cup soy milk	Add slowly, mixing with a whisk to form a smooth batter.
2 tablespoons sunflower oil	Add to the batter and whisk thoroughly.
1 teaspoon lemon juice	Add to the batter and mix well. Let stand for about 10 minutes before cooking.

HOW TO SPROUT BEANS

You can grow sprouts from several different types of bean, but they should be grown separately as they grow at different rates. Try sprouting mung beans, soybeans, brown or green lentils, aduki beans, chickpeas, and alfalfa seeds. The method used is the same for all types of beans.

Start a new jar every couple of days so that you have a continual supply. As they require sunlight, the sprouts will grow quite well on a kitchen surface, where it's easier to remember to rinse them, but they will not grow so big.

1 wide-necked jar

Beans or lentils to fill ⅓ of the jar, soaked overnight, then drained and rinsed well

Place in the jar.

Piece of fine-mesh material (e.g., new dishcloth or cheesecloth)
Elastic band

Cover the opening with the material and secure with the elastic band.

Lay the jar on its side and leave in a warm, dark place. Rinse the sprouts with lukewarm water at least 3 times a day. Try not to disturb the sprouts too much, as they may break. Drain off the water as thoroughly as you can (you don't need to remove the material).

After 3–4 days, your sprouts will be ready to eat. They will keep in the fridge in plastic bags for a few days.

NEUTRAL MUESLI

Oats are full of protein, vitamins, and minerals, making them an excellent energy-giving food. Their body-building properties lower blood sugar levels, nourish bones and teeth, and are vital for a healthy nervous system.

5 parts rice flakes
2 parts wheat germ
5 parts oats
1 part sliced almonds
1 part chopped hazelnuts
1 part sunflower seeds
1 part sesame seeds
1 part pumpkin seeds
1 part dried apricots, chopped
1 part dried figs, chopped
1 part raisins

You can make up as much muesli in advance as you wish and keep it in an airtight container.

raspberries
plums
soy milk

Serve with soy milk, topped with the fresh fruit. Soak the muesli in the soy milk for 10–20 minutes before serving.

OAT PASTRY DOUGH

Complete carbohydrates such as oats are perhaps the most efficient of foods in the Western diet. Use this oat pastry wherever recipes call for savory pie crust. The nutritional and healing properties of oats range from reducing cholesterol levels to strengthening the spleen and pancreas. They can be used where there is nervous weakness or a digestive problem. Makes 1 portion

2^1/$_4$ cups whole-wheat flour
a generous cup oats
^{1}/$_3$ cup ground almonds
^{1}/$_4$ cup sesame seeds
^{1}/$_2$ teaspoon dried thyme

Place in a large bowl.

1 teaspoon soy sauce
2^1/$_2$ tablespoons extra-virgin olive oil

Add to the bowl and rub together lightly with the fingertips until the mixture resembles fine breadcrumbs.

Gradually mix in cold water, a little at a time, until the dough binds together but is not too wet. Let it stand for 10 minutes.

Roll out the dough on a lightly floured surface. When it becomes difficult to roll, transfer it to a 12-inch nonstick tart pan or quiche pan, and push it into shape with your fingers.

Bake in the oven for 10 minutes, then remove from the oven and let it cool.

cooling foods

cooling foods

for hot people

Hot people feel hot, dislike heat, or are attracted to the cold. Too much heat in the body can be due to a number of factors such as:

- **eating too many warming foods (see page 8) and/or not enough cooling foods**
- **working very hard or being overactive**
- **over-consumption of alcohol, coffee, cigarettes, and synthetic drugs**
- **emotional stress**
- **fatigue**
- **exposure to an extremely hot climate**
- **an obstruction to an internal organ**

If you are a hot person, avoid foods that will heat you up even more. Stimulants such as coffee, alcohol, and sugar, and the overuse of heating spices, such as chili and pepper, should be avoided by a hot person. When cooling foods are eaten, the energy and fluids of the body are directed inwards and downwards so that the upper parts of the body cool down first. Hot people can eat some of the foods with neutral energy because they will not add further warmth to their bodies.

Some cooking techniques, like pressure-cooking, baking, and deep-frying can turn a cooling food into a warming food. Instead of using these methods, hot people should steam or simmer foods, and eat raw foods, which are more cooling than cooked food.

CALDO VERDE

Potato and cabbage are very detoxifying vegetables. Potatoes are mildly diuretic and help to neutralize body acids—great news for sufferers of arthritis and rheumatism. Cabbage is one of the best cures for many digestive problems, such as constipation and bloating. It contains compounds that studies have shown inhibit cancerous growths in the gastrointestinal tract. Serves 2

1 quart vegetable stock	Bring to a boil in a pot.
1 small onion, finely chopped **2 medium potatoes, sliced**	Add to the pot and simmer for 15 minutes.
2–3 dark green cabbage leaves, **cut in $\frac{1}{2}$-inch x $1\frac{1}{4}$-inch slices**	Add to the pot and simmer for another 15 minutes, until the vegetables are cooked.
1 tablespoon chopped oregano **2 teaspoons fresh lemon juice** **Dash of soy sauce**	Add to the pot and simmer for 5 more minutes. This soup is best served unblended but you may want to purée it for a smooth consistency.

GOLDEN BARLEY SOUP

Barley is a good source of B-complex vitamins, iron, calcium, phosphorus, and potassium. It is a great nourishing and strengthening grain with a strong diuretic effect. The high water content of bean sprouts makes them useful for flushing out toxins from the body. They also contain vitamin E, which promotes proper blood circulation. Serves 2

1 cup vegetable stock	Heat in a pot.
1 onion, finely chopped **1 stalk celery, finely chopped**	Add to the pot and simmer for 5 minutes.
3 tablespoons barley **Pinch of saffron** **Pinch of mixed herbs**	Add to the pot and simmer for 30 minutes.
1/3 cup rutabaga, diced **1 carrot, chopped** **1 1/2 cups vegetable stock**	Add to the pot, cover, and simmer for another 20 minutes, until the barley and vegetables are tender.
Dash of soy sauce **Ground black pepper** **Handful of mungbean sprouts**	Add to the pot, simmer for 2–3 minutes, and serve.

CREAMY MUSHROOM SOUP

Mushrooms help to neutralize the toxins created by our consumption of meat. They are also a rich source of germanium, which increases resistance to disease. Soy milk is the primary source of lecithin, a nutrient that helps to control and lower cholesterol. Celery has a high water content, which means it has few calories and is very alkalizing. Serves 2

1 small onion, sliced **1 small stalk celery, finely chopped** **1 tablespoon vegetable stock**	Place in a large pot and gently cook over low heat, covered, for 10 minutes, until the onion is softened.
1¹/₃ cups white mushrooms, **thinly sliced** **2 tablespoons vegetable stock** **¹/₂ teaspoon dried sage**	Add to the pot and stir. Cover and cook over low heat for another 10 minutes.
1 tablespoon soy sauce **2¹/₄ cups vegetable stock**	Add to the pot and bring to a boil. Simmer for 15 minutes.
1 heaping teaspoon cornstarch, **blended with a little cold water**	Remove the pot from the heat and let it cool for 2–3 minutes. Stir in the cornstarch mixture, then return to a very low heat to thicken.
2 tablespoons soy milk **Soy sauce, optional**	Add to the pot and simmer very gently for 2 minutes, stirring occasionally. Check the seasoning—you may wish to add some more soy sauce. This soup may be blended for a smoother texture.

CORN CHOWDER

Corn is packed with nutrients and enzymes, such as vitamin B3. The "extra" virgin status of olive oil means that it has less acidity than normal virgin oil and so is better quality. It also has a distinctive aromatic flavor. Serves 2

1 teaspoon extra-virgin olive oil **1 small onion, finely chopped** **1 small stalk celery, finely chopped**	Place in a large pot, covered, and cook over low heat gently for 6–7 minutes, until the onion is softened.
1/2 teaspoon ground coriander **1/2 zucchini, sliced** **2 fresh tomatoes, finely chopped**	Add to the pot, cover, and cook over low heat for 5 minutes.
14-ounce can corn, drained and well rinsed **3 cups vegetable stock** **2 teaspoons soy sauce**	Add to the pot and bring to a boil, then simmer for 20 minutes.
1 small handful of cilantro, chopped **Extra soy sauce, to taste** **Pinch of freshly ground black pepper**	Add to the pot and simmer for another 2–3 minutes, then remove from heat. Let cool for a few minutes, then purée to a creamy texture in a blender or food processor. Return to the pot to reheat.
Cilantro, for garnishing	Serve garnished.

CHILLED ASPARAGUS AND LEMON SOUP

Chinese nutritionists believe that asparagus "tones the yin." This means that it lubricates dryness in the body, making it good for conditions such as diabetes. Lemons stimulate the liver and gallbladder to eliminate toxins. Their acidity destroys the harmful bacteria that causes bloating, flatulence, and indigestion. Serves 2

10 ounces asparagus, trimmed and peeled	Cut off the tips and reserve. Cut into thin strips $^3/_4$–$1^1/_4$ inches long (to yield about $2^1/_2$ cups).
$^1/_2$ cup water	Heat in a pot.
1 small onion, finely chopped	Add to the pot, cover, and simmer gently for 5 minutes.
1 medium potato, peeled and diced **$3^1/_2$ cups water** **Salt and freshly ground black pepper**	Add to the pot with the asparagus strips and simmer for 10 minutes, until the potato and asparagus are very soft.
2 tablespoons chopped oregano **Juice of 1 lemon**	Add to the pot and simmer for 2–3 minutes, then purée in a blender or food processor. Steam the asparagus tips for 2–3 minutes until just tender, and add to the smooth soup.
Lemon zest, for garnishing	Chill, and serve garnished.

cooling foods

TOMATO, APPLE, AND CELERY SOUP

All the ingredients in this cleansing soup are alkalizing once they are digested. This means they are helpful in treating stress, which causes an acidic buildup in the body. Serves 2

1 teaspoon extra-virgin olive oil **2 stalks celery, chopped** **1 small onion, finely chopped**	Place in a large pot, covered, and cook over low heat for 10 minutes, until the onion is softened.
8 fresh tomatoes, puréed **1 dessert apple, peeled, cored, and diced** **1 teaspoon dried marjoram**	Add to the pot, bring to a boil, and simmer gently for 10 minutes.
2¹⁄₂ cups vegetable stock	Add to the pot, return to a boil, and simmer for 10 minutes.
Soy sauce, for serving	Serve immediately.

CLEANSING WATERCRESS SOUP

Watercress is an excellent cooling and nourishing tonic for mind and body. It is also a blood cleanser and is especially good when you feel stressed and run-down. Egyptian pharaohs gave watercress juice to their slaves twice a day, as they believed it would increase their productivity. Serves 2

1 cup vegetable stock	Heat in a large pot.
3–4 scallions, finely chopped **Pinch of ground nutmeg** **1/2 teaspoon dried thyme** **1 bay leaf**	Add to the pot, cover, and simmer for 5 minutes.
1 medium potato, peeled and sliced **2 cups vegetable stock**	Add to the pot, cover, and simmer for another 20 minutes, until the potato is cooked.
2 bunches of watercress, washed and roughly chopped **Pinch of sea salt or Kosher salt**	Add to the pot and simmer for 2 minutes.
1 cup soy milk	Turn off the heat and add. Stir well, and let stand for 5 minutes.
Freshly ground black pepper **Sprig of watercress, for garnishing**	Purée in a food processor or blender until smooth and creamy. Reheat in a pot, season, and serve garnished.

RAW YIN PURITY

The cooling properties in these ingredients are exceedingly healing. They have a moistening effect on the organs, so are useful for protection against inflammation, gastritis, hepatitis, and swollen glands. Cooling foods have therapeutic effects on headaches and depression, which can often be linked to an overheated liver that has begun to perform its cleansing and disease-fighting functions less efficiently.

apple

celery

chicory

pear

marjoram

broccoli

radish

Swiss chard

mungbean sprouts

spinach

cauliflower

(a very small amount of chives can be used for flavor)

There are no measurements as the idea is that you can make a very quick and simple salad using whatever you have available in your fridge, and that the quantities can be varied to give a different taste each time you make it.

This is the essence of detox, and this recipe should become a staple, being eaten as a snack and/or with meals.

It is best made using a meat grinder, but a food processor will do. Wash the vegetables and roughly chop them. Grind them in the grinder or put them in the food processor and blend until everything is chopped very finely. Scoop into a bowl and serve.

You can squeeze some fresh lemon juice over the salad to prevent it turning brown, if you wish. It will keep in the fridge for no more than a day.

cooling foods

AVOCADO AND STRAWBERRY SALAD

Food combining enables the proper digestion of different food groups. Fats and oils such as those found in avocados combine perfectly with the acidity of strawberries. When digested, they break down at a similar rate, allowing complete absorption of their nutrients into the body. Serves 2

1 ripe avocado, cut in half, pitted, peeled, and cut into cubes **6 strawberries, hulled and quartered**	Place in a bowl.
2 teaspoons lemon juice **2 teaspoons balsamic vinegar**	Pour on top and mix together gently.
Freshly ground black pepper	Season and serve.

AVOCADO, CHERRY TOMATO, AND SPINACH SALAD

All the ingredients in this salad improve vitality, due to the rich source of fats, protein, vitamin A, beta-carotene, and chlorophyll that they provide. Limes have an antiseptic quality and this, combined with the laxative actions of honey, help to purify the blood. Serves 2

1 ripe avocado, cut in half, pitted, peeled, and cubed

8 cherry tomatoes, cut in half

1 handful of baby spinach, washed, dried, and torn into pieces

Place in a salad bowl.

Juice of 1 lime

1 teaspoon honey

Pinch of sea salt or Kosher salt

Combine in a cup and pour over the salad. Mix gently and serve.

SOY MAYONNAISE

Soy is said to decrease cholesterol and prevent breast and ovarian cancer due to its phytoestrogen activity. Phytoestrogens are plant estrogens that have a positive effect on menopause and are generally helpful in ensuring reproductive health. Serves 2

1 cup soy milk

$1/2$ teaspoon sea salt or Kosher salt

$1/2$ teaspoon black pepper

$1/2$ teaspoon paprika

1 teaspoon dried basil

$1/4$ teaspoon whole-grain mustard

1 teaspoon honey

Place in a food processor and blend.

$\frac{2}{3}$ **cup extra-virgin olive oil**	Set the food processor to high speed and pour in the oil gradually. You will see the milk begin to emulsify.
2 teaspoons cider vinegar or white wine vinegar	Add and blend. This will give the mayonnaise a thicker consistency.

SNOWDRIFT SALAD

Cauliflower cleanses the blood of impurities and toxins and can also be beneficial for high blood pressure. Studies have shown that cauliflower has anticancerous and antioxidant compounds that protect against breast and colon cancer. This is a very light salad and may be served to accompany a main dish or other, more substantial, salads. Serves 2

1 small or $\frac{1}{2}$ large cauliflower, divided into small flowerets	Place in a blender or food processor and blend until the cauliflower resembles couscous. Transfer to a salad bowl.
10–15 seedless green grapes, cut in half	Add to the bowl and toss gently.
1-inch piece of cucumber, finely diced	
Juice of $\frac{1}{2}$ lemon, to taste	
Pinch of sea salt or Kosher salt, optional	

HERBY POLENTA CRACKERS

Polenta is cooked cornmeal. It is one of the most balanced starches and is very easy to digest. It has a diuretic effect, thereby helping the kidneys to excrete waste products and regulate proper digestion.

Makes 8 crackers

Preheat the oven to 350°F.

1¹/₂ cups boiling water	Bring to a boil in a small, tall-sided pan.
³/₄ cup medium polenta or cornmeal **1 teaspoon mixed dried herbs**	Add slowly, stirring continuously until you have the consistency of a smooth porridge.
¹/₂ teaspoon sea salt or Kosher salt **2 tablespoons soy margarine**	Remove the pan from the heat and add, mixing thoroughly. You may need to add a little extra water if the mixture is too stiff.

Spoon the batter onto very lightly greased nonstick baking sheets, spreading each spoonful into an even circle, then score each circle into triangles.

Bake in the oven for 20 minutes, or until the crackers are golden brown and crispy. Let cool on wire racks. Serve with dips and soups.

EGGPLANT AND CILANTRO DIP

Especially good for those who experience strong heat symptoms, this cooling snack cleanses the blood and protects against arterial damage made by the buildup of cholesterol. Serves 2

Preheat the oven to 375°F.

1 large eggplant

Bake whole with the stalk left on for 40 minutes, or until the skin has browned and it feels very soft to the touch. Let it cool, then peel.

1 garlic clove, crushed
¹/₂ teaspoon sea salt or Kosher salt
¹/₄ teaspoon ground black pepper
¹/₄ teaspoon ground cumin
1¹/₂ tablespoons extra-virgin olive oil

Place in a blender or food processor along with the eggplant flesh, and blend until smooth.

1 tablespoon chopped cilantro

Stir into the mixture and serve with flat bread (see page 90).

BLACKENED SAVOY, SNOW PEAS, AND BABY CORN WITH SESAME SEEDS AND LEMON

Vegetables are high in calcium and sesame is a good source of both calcium and protein, making this dish ideal for strengthening bones, teeth, and blood. Legumes contain almost as much protein as animal products, so this recipe is ideal for people who don't eat dairy foods. Serves 2

2 teaspoons sesame oil or extra-virgin olive oil	Using paper towels, wipe a wok or large frying pan with a thin coating of the oil, then heat over high heat for a few seconds.
2 large savoy cabbage leaves, cut into ¹/₂ x 1¹/₂ inch strips **12–14 snow peas** **6–8 whole baby corn, cut in half lengthwise**	Add to the pan and stir-fry until the vegetables begin to get blackened, 2–3 minutes.
1 teaspoon sesame seeds	Add to the pan and stir-fry for 30 seconds.
2–3 dashes soy sauce **2 teaspoons lemon juice**	Stir into the pan then cover for 1 minute to steam the vegetables. Serve hot or warm.

cooling foods

JAPANESE SPRING SALAD

Soybeans are unique among legumes in that they contain all eight essential amino acids, making them a perfectly balanced protein food. This dish will help to lower cholesterol and is also useful for post-menopausal women because of its plant estrogen content. Serves 2

²/₃ **cup dried soybeans, soaked overnight, or 1 cup canned beans**

Cook the drained beans in water until soft, for about 1 hour, then drain and let cool. If using canned beans, drain and rinse well. Place in a salad bowl.

4 ounces baby spinach leaf (about 2 large handfuls)
a handful of arugula

Tear into pieces, removing tough stalks, and add to the beans.

1 cup radishes, finely sliced
2 ounces snow peas (a small handful), sliced diagonally
1 mandarin orange, peeled and segmented

Add to the beans.

FOR THE DRESSING
4-oz. cake silken tofu
2 tablespoons orange juice
2 tablespoons soy sauce
2 teaspoons whole-grain mustard
2 teaspoons cider vinegar
Pinch of sea salt or Kosher salt
Freshly ground black pepper

Place all the ingredients in a blender or food processor and blend until smooth and creamy. Pour over the salad and gently mix together.

MIXED WHOLE-GRAIN SALAD, WITH MISO AND TARRAGON DRESSING

Whole-grains should make up about forty percent of our diet. Barley, groats (kashi), and millet protect against cancer and heart disease, while nourishing and soothing the digestive tract and liver. Miso is a fermented soybean paste that is high in protein and B12, a vitamin found mostly in meat and milk, making this salad an ideal choice for vegans. Serves 2

¹/₃ cup whole wheat berries, soaked for 12 hours and drained **¹/₃ cup whole-grain barley**	Bring a large pot of water to a boil and add the grains. Return to a boil and simmer for 50–60 minutes, until the grains are tender. Drain well and place in a bowl.
¹/₃ cup buckwheat groats (kashi)	Dry-roast in a pan over medium heat, until they give off a nutty aroma. Add plenty of water to cover, bring to a boil, and simmer for 10–15 minutes until tender. Drain well and add to the other grains.

FOR THE DRESSING
2 teaspoons brown miso
2 teaspoons cider vinegar
2 teaspoons soy sauce
1 teaspoon extra-virgin olive oil

Mix together and stir into the hot grains. As the grains cool down, they will absorb the dressing.

cooling foods

2 teaspoons sesame seeds, toasted

1 small carrot, peeled and grated

2-4 teaspoons raisins

1 tablespoon finely diced cucumber

1 small handful fresh tarragon, tough stalks removed, and roughly chopped

Place in a bowl and add to the grains once they are completely cool. Mix well and serve. You can add more miso for a stronger flavor.

CHICKPEA, POTATO, AND SPINACH SALAD WITH MINT YOGURT DRESSING

Chickpeas and potatoes are beneficial for the whole body, because of the high content of nutrients such as calcium, potassium, beta-carotene, folic acid, and vitamin C. In Chinese medicine, the subtle, bland flavor of the potato is believed to have a very calming effect on the digestive process. This makes it a tonic for digestive problems. Both potatoes and chickpeas neutralize acid and soothe inflammation in the body.

Serves 2

1½ cups cooked chickpeas

2 medium potatoes, cooked and diced

1 small handful fresh spinach, stalks removed, torn

Place in a bowl.

FOR THE DRESSING

1½ tablespoons plain yogurt

1 teaspoon tamarind juice

1 teaspoon honey

1 teaspoon finely chopped mint

Mix thoroughly until smooth and pour over the potato salad. Toss well.

1–2 mint leaves

Serve garnished.

MONGO-FILIPPINO MUNG BEANS WITH SPINACH AND TOMATO

This recipe is rich in iron, vitamins, and chlorophyll, which all have a very cooling and calming influence on the body and mind. Serves 2

¹/₂ **cup dried mung beans, rinsed** **2¹/₄ cups water** **1 bay leaf**	Place in a pot and bring to a boil. Boil for 2 minutes, then turn down the heat and simmer for 1–1¹/₂ hours, until the beans are tender and almost mushy.
1 tablespoon extra-virgin olive oil **1 garlic clove, crushed** **1 small onion, finely chopped**	Fry gently in a frying pan until the onion is soft and golden.
1 medium tomato, peeled and chopped	Add, and fry gently until all the excess liquid is gone. Add to the mung beans and simmer for 5 minutes, stirring occasionally.
2 large handfuls spinach, washed, drained, and coarsely chopped **2 teaspoons lime juice** **Pinch of sea salt or Kosher salt**	Add to the beans and simmer until the spinach is cooked, about 5 minutes.
2 wedges of lime, for garnishing	Serve with rice or millet, garnished.

cooling foods

CORN ENCHILADAS FILLED WITH TOFU, SPINACH, AND SALSA

Tofu contains lots of vitamin B12, an essential nutrient often deficient in vegetarians. Its cooling nature helps to relieve inflammation of the stomach and neutralizes toxins in the body. Serves 2

Preheat the oven to 375°F.

9 ounces smoked tofu, sliced

Place on a nonstick baking tray and brown under a medium broiler, turning once. Let cool and set aside.

1 teaspoon extra-virgin olive oil
2 handfuls spinach leaves, chopped
1¹/₂ tablespoons soy sauce

Using paper towels, wipe a wok or large frying pan with the oil. Add the spinach and soy sauce to the wok with the tofu. Stir-fry for 2–3 minutes over medium heat, then remove from heat and set aside.

FOR THE SALSA
6 tomatoes, skinned and chopped
1 small onion
¹/₄ teaspoon ground cumin
1 handful cilantro, chopped
Juice of ¹/₂ lime
Pinch of sea salt or Kosher salt
Freshly ground black pepper
2 teaspoons extra-virgin olive oil

Place in a blender or food processor and blend until quite finely chopped.

4 corn taco shells

Divide the spinach mixture among the taco shells and place on their sides in an ovenproof dish. Cover with the salsa, and bake in the oven for about 30 minutes until heated through.

¹/₂ avocado, sliced, for garnishing
Cilantro, for garnishing

Garnish and serve hot, with a side salad.

MARINATED GRILLED VEGETABLES

It is important to consume vegetables daily for their therapeutic high-fiber, low-fat qualities. Marinating and grilling vegetables accentuates their full flavor and brings out their healing properties. Serves 2

FOR THE MARINADE
1 tablespoon extra-virgin olive oil
1 tablespoon balsamic vinegar
Freshly ground black pepper
Pinch of salt
1 teaspoon honey
2 teaspoons lemon juice

Mix and set aside.

1 eggplant, sliced into ½-inch circles
1 red pepper, cut in half lengthwise, cored, and seeded
1 red onion, sliced lengthwise
2 zucchini, sliced lengthwise, ¼-inch thick
6 cherry tomatoes
4 asparagus spears, trimmed

Place under a hot broiler until the vegetables begin to blacken and are soft. The red pepper should be cooked skin-side up. Remove from the heat and let cool. Peel off the red pepper skin and cut into strips. Place the vegetables in a bowl.

Small handful of oregano, chopped
Small handful of basil, chopped
Small handful of parsley, chopped
14-ounce can kidney beans, drained and rinsed

Add to the bowl. Pour in the marinade and mix well. Let it marinate for 1–2 hours.

This recipe is very good served with flatbread (see page 90).

TOFU AND PINEAPPLE STIR-FRY

Tofu contains as much calcium as milk and is very low in calories. Pineapples have a strong diuretic action which helps the detoxification process; they also contain an enzyme that aids proper digestion. Serves 2

FOR THE SAUCE

1 small can pineapple chunks	Place in a food processor or blender and blend until smooth.
1 red chili, seeded and finely chopped	
1 garlic clove, crushed	
1-inch piece ginger root, peeled and finely grated	
2 tablespoons soy sauce	
2 tablespoons cider vinegar	
1 teaspoon cornstarch	
4$\frac{1}{2}$ ounces plain tofu, cut into cubes	Broil for 5 minutes under medium heat until golden brown.
2 teaspoons extra-virgin olive oil	Heat in a wok or large frying pan until hot.
2 scallions, sliced	Add to the wok and stir-fry for 2 minutes.
$\frac{1}{4}$ red pepper, seeded and sliced	
$\frac{1}{2}$ carrot, sliced in strips	
$\frac{1}{2}$ zucchini, sliced diagonally	Add and stir-fry for 2 minutes.
12 snow peas	
1 handful of bean sprouts	Add to pan, along with the grilled tofu. Stir-fry for 1 minute.
1 handful of sliced Napa cabbage	
1 tablespoon chopped cilantro	Add the sauce and cilantro. Cook for 3 minutes until bubbling.

SPAGHETTI WITH CLAMS

In Chinese medicine, clams are used to moisten dryness, nurture the yin, and resolve damp conditions, such as thrush and bloating. This recipe is effective for fluid retention, and helps to soften hard lumps in the body, such as kidney and gallstones. Serves 2

1 pound fresh clams, well scrubbed **¹/₂ cup water**	Put in a pot and cook until the shells open, about 3–5 minutes. Drain, reserving the water. Discard any shells that are still closed. Remove the clam meat from the shells and set aside.
1 tablespoon extra-virgin olive oil **1 garlic clove, cut in half lengthwise**	Fry gently in a heavy pan for 3–4 minutes, then remove the garlic and discard it.
14-oz. can chopped tomatoes	Add, along with the reserved clam stock, and simmer for 20–25 minutes.
¹/₂ pound spaghetti	Cook until *al dente* as instructed on the package.
¹/₂ tablespoon chopped fresh parsley **2 teaspoons fresh lemon juice** **Pinch of sea salt or Kosher salt**	Add to the sauce along with the clams, and cook for 1 minute.
Freshly ground black pepper	Pile the spaghetti onto serving plates, season, and spoon the clam sauce on top. Serve immediately.

CRAB AND ORANGE WRAPPED IN SWISS CHARD LEAVES

Crab meat contains calcium, phosphorous, iron, vitamins A, B1, B2, and niacin, giving it a strong detoxifying and anti-inflammatory effect on the body. Swiss chard is a beneficial aid to the digestive system. Serves 2

2 freshly cooked crabs	Remove the meat from the shells, separating the dark and white meat.
FOR THE SAUCE **Juice of ½ lemon** **Juice of ½ orange** **½ cup fish or vegetable stock**	Place in a food processor or blender, along with the dark crab meat, and blend to make a smooth sauce. Warm gently in a pan.
6 large Swiss chard leaves, stalks removed	Blanch one at a time in boiling water for 5–10 seconds, then immediately put them into cold water. Let them dry for a few moments. Handle very carefully so as not to break the leaves.
Pinch of turmeric **Pinch of cayenne** **Pinch of sea salt or Kosher salt** **Freshly ground black pepper**	Add to the white crabmeat and mix gently.
1-inch piece ginger root, peeled and grated	Gather it into your hand and squeeze the juice over the white crabmeat.
Chopped chives	Lay the leaves out flat and divide the white crabmeat among the leaves, placing it in the center. Sprinkle a little chopped chives on each filling and carefully fold over the sides and then the ends. Steam the stuffed leaves for no more than 2 minutes. Pour the sauce over them and serve with boiled rice, with a little coconut milk mixed into the boiling water.

cooling foods

MILLET PILAF WITH BAKED EGGPLANT

Millet—sometimes called the "queen of the grains"—has been eaten for thousands of years by the people of Africa, India, and the Far East. Eggplants are rich in bioflavonoids which help to renew arteries and prevent strokes and hemorrhages. Serves 2

Preheat the oven to 350°F.

FOR THE PILAF

2 teaspoons extra-virgin olive oil
1 small onion

Gently fry, covered, for 4–5 minutes, until the onion is softened.

1 teaspoon ground coriander
2 cloves garlic, crushed

Add to the pan and fry for another 5 minutes.

2 teaspoons pitted black olives
³/₄ cup millet

Add to the pan and fry for another 2 minutes, until the millet starts to give off a nutty aroma.

14-oz. can chopped tomatoes
1³/₄ cups vegetable stock

Add to the pan, bring to a boil, and simmer for 20 minutes, uncovered. If the millet still has a slight bite you may need to add some extra water and cook a little longer.

2 teaspoons slivered almonds, toasted
2–3 dashes soy sauce
1 tablespoon chopped parsley

Add when the millet is tender, then remove from the heat.

FOR THE EGGPLANTS

**1 medium eggplant, cut in
¹/₂-inch slices**

1 tablespoon olive oil

Arrange the slices in an ovenproof dish and spread the olive oil over them so each slice is thinly coated. Cover, and bake for 10 minutes.

1 tablespoon tahini

1 tablespoon water

juice of ¹/₂ lemon

1 garlic clove, crushed

1 teaspoon soy sauce

Mix in a small bowl. Remove the eggplant slices from the oven and stir the mixture into them, coating the slices well. Return to the oven and bake uncovered for another 15 minutes or until the slices are soft and tender.

To serve, spoon the pilaf onto serving plates and top with the eggplant mixture.

SIMPLICITY SUSHI

Salmon is low in cholesterol, has a high protein content, and is easily digestible. It is a rich source of essential omega-3 fatty acids that help to maintain skin, teeth, and nails. Nori, a sea vegetable, is high in protein and nutrients that help reduce cholesterol. Serves 2

1¼ cups sushi rice or short-grain rice	Soak in cold water for 15 minutes, rinse, and drain.
2 cups water	Place in a pot with the rice and bring to a boil. Stir once and cover, reduce heat to very low, and leave for 10 minutes. Turn off the heat and let it stand, covered, for 5 minutes.
¼ cup rice wine vinegar or white wine vinegar **1 teaspoon sugar** **1 teaspoon sea salt or Kosher salt**	Heat gently in a pan. Spread the rice on a large plate or tray and pour the vinegar mixture over it. Stir with a fork for 5 minutes, making sure that all the rice is coated in vinegar. Let it cool, then divide in half.
2 sheets nori seaweed	Toast quickly under a broiler or over a gas flame. You will see the color change.
⅓ cup crabmeat **Thin strips of cucumber** **1 teaspoon sesame seeds, toasted**	Place the nori sheets on 2 pieces of plastic wrap. Using one half of the sushi rice, divide it between the nori sheets and spread it evenly over each sheet. Place a line of crabmeat, a few strips of cucumber, and a few sesame seeds down the center, and roll up each sheet. Wrap in plastic wrap and chill.

Make 8–10 molds by cutting the cardboard inner tube of a paper towel roll into 1-inch sections, and line them with foil or plastic wrap.

3 ounces smoked salmon (lox)
Wasabi (Japanese horseradish)

Press the remaining rice into the molds. Cut the smoked salmon into 1¹/₂-inch pieces. Take a piece of smoked salmon, thinly spread a little of the wasabi paste over it, and push it down on top of the rice. Chill.

TO SERVE
Dark soy sauce
Wasabi
Pickled ginger

To serve, remove the molds. Remove the plastic wrap from the sushi rolls and cut them into slices. Arrange with the salmon sushi and serve.

YIN FRUIT SALAD

A raw fruit salad is an excellent way of preserving the nutrients in food. The fruits in this dish are rich in water-soluble B-complex and C vitamins, but these can be easily lost through careless storage. An excess of exposure to air, water, heat, and light will rob fresh fruit of its essential goodness, so buy in season and eat when fully ripe. Serves 2

1 banana	Chop into a bowl.
1/2 apple	
6–8 blueberries	
1/2 pear	
1-inch slice watermelon	
1 tangerine	
2–3 strawberries	
2/3 cup orange and grapefruit juice, mixed in equal parts	Pour over the fruit.
1 tablespoon yogurt, for serving	Serve topped with the yogurt.

cooling foods

GOOSEBERRY FOOL

Gooseberries help the liver to eradicate waste products. They also contain digestive enzymes that promote the proper and complete breakdown of protein. This pudding is a therapeutic treat. Serves 2

1 cup fresh gooseberries, topped and tailed	Place in a pan, bring to a boil, and simmer until tender.
2 tablespoons honey or apple juice concentrate	
2 tablespoons fresh orange juice	
4-ounce cake plain tofu	Blend in a blender or food processor and then add the gooseberries.
½ teaspoon lemon juice	Purée until the texture is quite smooth. Serve chilled in dessert glasses.
1 tablespoon sunflower oil	

COOLING MUESLI

The grains in this muesli are calming and focusing for the mind and body—the perfect way to start the detox day! Make sure that you purchase sun-dried rather than sulphur-dried fruits.

3 parts wheat flakes	You can make up as much muesli in advance as you wish, and keep it in an airtight container.
1 part wheat germ	
4 parts millet flakes	
1 part slivered almonds	
1 part sunflower seeds	
1 part dried apple	
1 part dried pear	
fresh banana	Serve with soy milk, topped with the fresh fruit. Soak the muesli in the soy milk for 10–20 minutes before serving.
soy milk	

BANANA AND CASHEW SLICE

Bananas are antifungal and are a natural antibiotic. They detoxify by encouraging the production of the beneficial bacteria in the intestinal tract. Nuts are generously packed with an abundance of vitamins and minerals. They are high in protein and essential fatty acids, which are required for most bodily functions.

Makes 8 slices

Preheat the oven to 375°F.

¹/₄ cup sunflower oil
2 medium bananas (about
   ¹/₂ pound)
¹/₂ teaspoon vanilla extract
1 teaspoon ground cinnamon
¹/₄ teaspoon ground cardamom

Blend in a blender or food processor.

¹/₂ cup cashews

Add and blend for a few seconds to break them up.

1 cup dry, unsweetened coconut
¹/₂ cup oats
1 apple, peeled and grated

Add and blend for a few seconds.

Pour into a greased 9-inch baking pan. Bake in the oven for 25–30 minutes. Let cool, then cut into wedges.

MILLET AND APRICOT PUDDING

Apricots are bursting with antioxidants, which have been shown to prevent cholesterol buildup in the arteries. Millet is an alkaline grain that is beneficial for combating stress. Serves 2

Preheat oven to 350°F.

¾ cup millet

Toast in a dry frying pan over medium heat, until it begins to change color and give off a nutty aroma.

½ cup apple juice
½ cup orange juice
1 cup water

Add to the pan, cover, and simmer for 30 minutes until the millet is soft and the mixture the consistency of porridge. You may need to add more water to prevent it from drying out.

4 fresh apricots, pitted and roughly chopped
1 tablespoon honey
½ cup soy milk
Pinch of ground cinnamon

Stir into the pan, then scoop into an ungreased ovenproof dish with a lid. Bake in the oven for 30 minutes.

¼ cup slivered almonds

Place on a baking sheet and toast under a medium broiler until golden brown.

Honey, for serving

Serve the pudding hot, topped with the almonds and a little honey.

POACHED PEARS WITH HONEY AND PISTACHIOS

Poaching pears brings out their pectin content. Pectins bond to toxins and cholesterol in the body to facilitate their elimination. Pistachios cleanse the blood and are a tonic for the liver and kidneys. Serves 2

1¼ cups water **3 tablespoons honey** **½ cinnamon stick** **1 clove** **1 vanilla bean or ½ teaspoon vanilla** **extract** **Juice of ½ lemon** **Juice of ½ orange**	Heat in a pan just big enough to stand the pears in—they should be covered by the syrup.
2 large plump pears, peeled and **cored but left whole**	Poach without boiling for 10–15 minutes until soft. The time needed will depend on the ripeness of the pears. Remove the pears and set aside. Reduce the syrup until quite thick, then remove from the heat and cool.
1 tablespoon chopped, unsalted **pistachios, for decoration**	Put pears on serving dishes and cover with the syrup. Decorate and serve.

STRAWBERRY AND RASPBERRY CHEESECAKE

Strawberries eliminate harmful toxins from the blood, making them ideal as a skin-cleansing food. Raspberries have an astringent quality, which helps to clear mucus and catarrh. They also help to relieve the pain of excess menstrual flow and muscle cramps. Serves 2

½ pound low-fat, low-sugar, oatmeal cookies	Place in a food processor and blend to a fine crumb.
⅓ cup soy margarine	Melt in a pan, then add to the cookies and blend briefly. Press the mixture into a 10-inch fluted tart pan or quiche pan, and refrigerate for 20 minutes to set.
1¼ pounds soft tofu **1 teaspoon vanilla extract**	Place in a blender or food processor, and blend until smooth.
2 tablespoons concentrated strawberry and apple juice, or raspberry and apple, or rice syrup **⅛ teaspoon powdered agar agar**	Heat the liquid in a pan and add the agar agar. Bring to a gentle simmer, stirring continuously until the grainy texture of the agar agar disappears. Add to the tofu and blend together. Pour immediately over the cookie base and spread evenly. Refrigerate for 15 minutes to set.
½ pound of all-fruit (no sugar or sweetener) jam	Heat in a pan until melted and pour evenly over the cheesecake.
1 cup fresh strawberries and raspberries, mixed	Arrange on top and let cool until set.

STRAWBERRY AND RASPBERRY SMOOTHIE

The acid and vitamin C in these fruits helps to cleanse the body of toxins. These red berries also help to relieve the symptoms of conditions that affect the urinary system, such as painful urination or the inability to urinate. Serves 1

10 raspberries
6 strawberries
1 banana
Juice of 1 orange
10 ice cubes

Blend well in a blender and serve immediately.

APPLE, PEAR, AND MINT JUICE

Research shows that these fruits can actually remove radioactive residue and toxic heavy metals from the digestive system. Apples and pears are excellent sources of pectin—a water-soluble fiber that binds to toxins in the system and helps their excretion from the body. Mint has a calming effect on digestion, protecting against stomach gas and destroying internal parasites. Makes 1 large glass

2 apples	Choose your favorite varieties of apples and pears, quarter them, and
2 pears	push them through a juicing machine along with the mint. Serve
3–4 stems of fresh mint	immediately.

MELON, PEAR, AND CELERY JUICE

Melon removes toxins while rehydrating the body with its highly-alkaline mineral content. It requires little digestion and passes through the system quickly. Celery reduces acid buildup and purifies the bloodstream. The iodine content in pears helps to regulate the body's metabolism. Pears are also high in fiber, which makes this juice a good tonic for clearing obstructed bowels. Makes 1 large glass

½ honeydew melon	Push through a juicing machine.
3 pears	
1 stick celery	
10 ice cubes	Place in a blender or food processor, add the juice, and blend together. Serve immediately.

cooling foods

CANTALOUPE MELON WITH ORANGE AND MINT

Melon and orange juice require little digestion, so are ideal if you need a quick energy boost. Melons are high in silica and nutrients that tone and insulate the nerve fibers. Mint contains menthol, which enhances digestion and has an antispasmodic effect that eases digestive pain. Makes 1 large glass

1 cantaloupe melon, cut in half and seeded	Place the halves in serving bowls.
1 orange, peeled, thinly sliced, and cut into quarters **Juice of 1 orange** **10 mint leaves, finely chopped**	Mix in a bowl. Pile the mixture into the melon halves and pour any remaining juice on top. Serve chilled.

BANANA AND MANGO SMOOTHIE

Bananas are beneficial for dry conditions in the body, such as dry coughs and tight sensations in the chest. Mangoes have an immense blood-cleansing capacity that counteracts acidity and reduces the heat brought on by fever. Makes 1 large glass

2 bananas **1/2 mango** **15 ice cubes** **Juice of 1 orange**	Place in a food processor or blender and blend until very smooth. Serve in a chilled glass.

index

bibliography

Kloss, J., *Back to Eden*, Back to
Eden Publishing Co., 1992
McKeith, G., *Living Food for
Health*, Piatkus, 2000
Onstadt, D., *Wholefoods
Companion*, Chelsea Green, 1996
Pitchford, P., *Healing with
Wholefoods*, North Atlantic
Books, 1993

acknowledgments

Louisa J. Walters would like to
thank Lawrence and Sarah
Dawkin-Jones, Will Hancock,
and Chris Rollinson for helping
to test out recipes.
Aliza Baron Cohen would like to
thank Alexis, Helen, and all her
family for their support and
encouragement, and the
(unborn) baby for inspiration.
Adrian Mercuri would like to
thank his parents, Antonio and
Marisa, and his brothers Jeff,
Daniel, and Renato, for all their
love and support.

bliss creative
health centre

can be contacted at:
333 Portobello Road
London W10 5SA
tel: 020 8969 3331